GRAVE CLOTHES:
A NOVEL ABOUT THE DEATH OF LAZARUS

Elaine Rose Penn

© Copyright 2011, Elaine Rose Penn

All Rights Reserved.

No part of this book may be reproduced, stored in a retrieval system, or transmitted by any means, electronic, mechanical, photocopying, recording, or otherwise, without written permission from the author.

ISBN: 978-0-9700449-4-5

Other books by Elaine Rose Penn:
Soul Ties
A Chance At Life: Stories of Inspiration and Hope for Adoptive and Foster Parents
My Soul Looks Back and Wonders: The Call of God on a Woman's Life
When Kingdoms Fall: A Novel About the Fall of Lucifer

I am the Resurrection and the Life:
he that believeth in me, though he were dead, yet shall he live: and whosoever liveth and believeth in me shall never die. Believest thou this?

CHAPTER ONE

A strange thing happened at the tomb of Lazarus on the day his sisters buried him for a second time.

In the midst of the jostling crowd of mourners stood two cloaked, mysterious figures who had traveled great distances to get there for the funeral. Although many others had come only to see if the rumor which persisted during his life was true, one of the two came truly to honor him. They measured their movements carefully with those of the swelling processional and took every precaution necessary to hide their identities from prying eyes. One of the strangers was a woman in the early autumn of her life. The deeply etched lines around her eyes and mouth belied her actual age and made her appear more burdened by life than she really was. Still, the lines were there for a reason.

The other was a much older man, but not too many years the junior of the man before whose tomb he now stood. Though he too had physically aged quickly before his time, there was something of a strange kind of stateliness in the way that he comported himself that made one stop to wonder at what could possibly be its source. They each, including Lazarus, had made these peculiar sojourns into each other's lives mostly out of an unstated loyalty and had, on more than one occasion, stood looking on from afar as uninvited albeit obligatory compatriots. They secretly needed each other in a way that few could possibly understand, yet they were also careful to preserve the imposed distance between themselves for fear that a covenant was somehow not allowed.

The man looked up first, momentarily disclosing his identity as his cloak fell away from his face. He succeeded in catching the eye of the younger woman who was the daughter of Jairus, a once prominent head of a synagogue located in the city of Capernaum. He hoped that on this occasion at least that she would allow him the privilege of her thoughts and feelings. She, fearing the crowd's recognition by association, nodded a subtle greeting of recognition but then just as quickly averted her eyes. Although they knew each other well by both name as well as life's journey, they had never exchanged a single word between them.

The man from Nain and the younger woman from Capernaum now exchanged furtive glances at each other, and then in unison peered forlornly at the tomb of Lazarus. The two reached the same solemn conclusion as the crowd. This time, Lazarus was dead for good. And since the three had never spoken, these two would never hear the third tell his story in his own words. They would only have the rumors that Lazarus himself had perpetuated.

"You! I know you! Are you not Hadassah, the daughter of Jairus of Capernaum?"

Someone was in the face of the woman from Capernaum, pointing a finger and drawing the attention of those who stood close by.

"You are wrong. I am oft mistaken for her. My name is Azaiah of Bethany!" she snapped at the intruder as she pulled the cloak tightly around her face and head and wedged herself into the mass of mourners whose wailing and contrived weeping provided a perfect shield.

But then a similar thing happened to the man from Nain.

Just as Hadassah was sure that she had eluded detection, a heated exchange broke out just a few feet in front of her which appeared to involve the pushing and shoving of several men. Her heart stopped momentarily when she realized that the skirmish seemed centered around the spot where the man from Nain had been standing when he nodded to her just moments before. In a rush of panic, and without thinking, she pushed her way towards the older man fearing that he might get trampled in the foray. The press of the crowd provided the momentum she needed to get to him, and before she realized what was happening, the throng parted company to clear a place for her right next to the man, whom, like herself, had been raised from the dead. He was known as Josiah, the son of the deceased widow of Nain.

The entire mass of heaving, shrieking, bawling mourners became eerily still and silent as if on cue, with their shared focus on the two strangers who stood before them. The blood drained from Hadassah's face as she continued in her clumsy efforts to hide her face, but this time with her hands. Josiah stood beside her stoic and stubborn, and for added effect, dramatically yanked his cloak free from his face. The silence of the crowd all at once became a concerted gasp of recognition, and Josiah decided that he would be the first to speak.

As Josiah lifted his voice for all to hear, he shoved Hadassah behind him in a protective gesture and grasped the edges of her cloak as he did so to aid her in hiding her face.

"Lazarus was a friend of mine, as he was of yours! As you have surely recognized by now, I am Josiah of Nain," yelled Josiah.

The crowd reacted immediately to the news that a celebrity now stood in touching distance. Josiah continued to cry out as he stepped strategically away from Hadassah to widen the distance between them.

"I have come to mourn the death of this our beloved friend," he continued to shout above the din of the clamoring multitude.

"I have done so out of subtlety because I did not wish to draw attention to myself. It is Lazarus who is deserving of our attention and respect today. Please allow me to go my way in peace."

The throng was completely swayed by the ruse as they stared at the man who was as famous as Lazarus. Hadassah took the opportunity to duck her way backwards into the throng of people who now surged forward to get a better look at Josiah. As she had on many occasions very similar to this one, she bowed herself low to the ground as she passed through the throng - hobbling and running in a grotesque, bent posture for the purpose of escaping as well as to hide her face. For just a moment, someone – an elderly woman - deliberately stepped out and blocked her path. She looked up in an instant, and locked eyes with the woman who had initially recognized her and called out her name. The woman, inexplicably, stepped aside to allow her to pass. They would meet again under a most unusual set of circumstances, but for today and for this moment, neither of them could know that their meeting at this tomb was not by chance. The woman, who was now far advanced in her years, was none other than Sarah, the daughter of Hezron, who had been healed of a twelve year long issue of blood many years before.

Once Hadassah found the safer dirt roads leading north back toward Galilee, she spoke a heart-felt prayer in gratitude for her comrade Josiah who had risked his own safety for hers. She was a jumble of conflicting emotions as she tried with controlled breathing to make her heart stop racing. She had stopped running now but still maintained a brisk pace as she made her way slowly down the familiar paths leading away from the ancient, towering catacombs above her. Her thoughts went – as they had many, many times before – to that day many years ago when she died as a young girl. Of the three, she had been the first.

Unlike Lazarus, she had never awakened to the cold of marble holding her up from the insides of a dark, fetid tomb. There were certain aspects about having died, however, that she would never forget until the day she died again. Her first memory was that of the shrieks and cries of the mourners. Although the intense and macabre chorus of their wailing shoved her back through the chasm too quickly, the fixed gulf held without shattering.

Momentarily, though, something caught her, as if by her hand, and pulled her gently through the last few inches of the way. It was a strong hand and familiar as well, and it seemed to guide her past a point in the chasm where something in her spirit seemed to recoil and not want to go further. The hand gripped her with a greater insistence and assurance, and seemed to communicate that she had no other choice but to yield. Something in her spirit capitulated, but she would never escape the nagging sensation that she shouldn't have given in.

She was a girl of twelve, just entering womanhood by Jewish standards, and though she remembered falling sick, the details of her terminal illness had long been swallowed up by the infamy of her resurrection. She could not even bring back to her recollection the pain of the dying process. Because of this, the memory of the miracle did not start with her death, but rather with her rebirth. Her father, Jairus, had regaled her – even tormented her for years and years with the retelling of the wonderful miracle, but for her, all she could remember was awaking out of sleep to the sound of wailing and the touch of the Master's hand.

When she found herself on the earth side of the chasm, staring into the face of the Healer from Nazareth, she had a vivid memory of never having been so hungry before in her life.

"Give her something to eat," was the gentle command of the Master to her parents.

The low and haunting wail of the mourners could still be heard just outside of her bedroom door, and she heard the Master give stern warning to her parents about discussing the details of her resurrection with anyone outside of their household. She often wondered what her life could have been like if they had simply obeyed Him. There were other people in the room besides her parents, and later she would learn that these others were Peter, James, and John, the disciples of Jesus.

As she reflected, she also remembered the great sadness she saw in the eyes of the Healer. It was as if He already knew what her new life would be like. She remembered how the mourners filled her tiny bedroom and stared at her when she came out of the chasm. Some touched her, willing to believe in the miracle. Others kept calling her name, *Hadassah! Hadassah!* as if the test of her response would prove that she was in fact alive. Still others banded together secretly and accused her parents of deceit. A group of them had just laughed in the face of the Healer when He told them that she was not dead – only asleep.

As she walked along in deep contemplation about the issue of death, she reflected to herself that yes, *torment*, was the best word to describe the many questions that had flown past her head about the grave. A spirit of sadness settled in about her soul as she realized the irony that although she had regained life on that day as a young girl, she also lost herself as a person with future hopes and dreams. From that day forward, she became an object to be scrutinized and studied. It seemed as though her past life – everything earlier than her twelfth year - disappeared into that chasm from which she had reluctantly been pulled.

When queried incessantly about what death had been like, what she had seen, and what she had felt, she always found herself flustered and speechless. And then the inevitable would happen. She would get those looks. The first look led to the question, "If indeed you died why have you no details or ready report to give about what you saw?" The first look would then spawn the second look, even though she never spoke a word in response to the first query. The second question was always, *"Did you see Father Abraham?"* Then, Jairus, ever the elder and synagogue teacher, would jump in to salvage her waning credibility as an eyewitness to death by answering for her. He would offer up the most marvelous renditions of what he believed she'd seen with made-up stories of how she'd lain in the bosom of Father Abraham and what a wonderful experience that had been.

If the questioner had been thoughtful enough to bring along a generous offering of lentils, olives, pomegranates, apples or flax, the ruler of the synagogue would add layers of additional details and paint them with sights and sounds. Hadassah would nod at all of this, giving her assent to his fabrications. If ever she hesitated, the questioners would always look back to Jairus for a confirmation of his self-styled reporting, as if he had been the one who had died and come back rather than she. He, on the other hand, seemed to relish these grand performances, and would feign some burden in the retelling as if to stoke the donations. The preposterous stories made up by Jairus about what she had witnessed of paradise while dead, grew so fantastic that it was often the case that he would forget the embellishment of a previous report, and have to issue a much grander testimony so to make up for an omission.

The fact is, except for the screeching and screaming of the mourners, and that hand that belonged to the Man from Galilee, Hadassah remembered nothing else. How many times had she tortured herself trying to grab the images and shadows that inched along like climbing vines about her memories? Some days she could remember some things, but only fleetingly, and they seemed to grow fainter with time. Other things, like light which was brighter than the noonday sun, singing in melodies of the purest harmony, faces of people, angels, and other-worldly creatures, and peals and peals of unbridled laughter - she could remember better but still dimly. Even these would scramble away before she could take a hold of them for reflection and further examination.

The conspiracy of silence was one way of winning and keeping her father's heart as he became the sought-after eyewitness rather than she, but as the days and weeks turned into years, even Jairus stopped seeing her as a person in need of love and affirmation. The loss of their privacy and home life seemed to alienate her from her mother as well as the other women in her life. Her mother Azaiah would turn on her at the smallest infraction, as more and more, Hadassah could be victimized for leaving their home to do even the simplest tasks. In her mother's mind, her daughter became the pawn of her father's deceit.

Increasingly, their lives became centered on a constant stream of visitors whose loved ones were near death or in recent death. It became a sort of perverse family business to provide comfort and education about what would come next in the afterlife for a parade of dead daughters, husbands, wives, sons, fathers, and sisters. The day came when Azaiah could take it no more, and began to take out her frustrations on her young daughter. It was on that day that her mother spoke the words that would forever ring in Hadassah's soul.

"We have had no peace in this home since the day that you came back from the dead!"

As soon as Azaiah said it, the pent-up emotion seemed to spin itself out, and she regretted that such a truth could be so mean as well.

Hadassah tried to discipline herself over the years to not embark upon this reverie too often. It caused her great melancholy which she found next to impossible to shake once she had given herself leave to go too deep. She sighed sorrowfully at the memories – it seemed that she had lived most of her life thinking these exact same thoughts. And always, without fail, she would leave this mental state of another place and time with the private verdict that her mother had most likely been right. She should have stayed dead.

From a small distance behind her, a voice broke through her musing which startled her, and because she had hurried through life rather than walking, she did a most natural thing. She took off running as if someone were in pursuit.

"Wait! Hadassah! It is me, Josiah! Please, wait just a moment. I will not hurt you!" cried out Josiah.

The younger woman began gasping for air as she ran for dear life, and before she knew it she'd lost her footing and soon felt the sharp pain of a stone which cut deeply into one of her knees as she fell. Her cry of pain and anguish cut the heart of the older man from Nain, and momentarily he wished he had not tried to follow her. But he needed her desperately – as much as she needed him.

Josiah, though a man of some age, was able to cover the distance between them rather quickly and stooped to gather Hadassah in his arms. Before she would agree to his comfort, however, she looked quickly about to see if he had been followed. She couldn't forget that less than an hour ago, she had almost been mauled because of her association to him. After she took note of the fact that the roads were empty, she fell into his chest sobbing deeply and wept like a small child.

As Josiah held on to her and allowed her this rare freedom, he began to muse to himself about what a strange day this had turned out to be. He had started this day with the intent to pay final homage to his good friend Lazarus as anonymously as possible. He had anticipated that Hadassah would be there because the three of them were always there for each other. He had even anticipated how risky it might be if someone recognized either of them in the crowd of mourners. He figured that if either of them were discovered, he would do whatever was necessary to wrench the unpleasant attention away from the younger woman from Capernaum. He could handle the pointing and gawking, he figured. He had been handling it nearly all of what remained of his life after his resurrection. Never, however, in a million years could he have anticipated these strange turn of events happening in of all places at the tomb of Lazarus.

When the tears were spent, Hadassah looked up into the eyes of Josiah, but continued sobbing. She felt weary in her soul, and reflected just for a moment on the fact that with the exception of the Master's hand, she rarely experienced moments like this when she felt so safe in the midst of turmoil. Josiah took his own hand and tenderly wiped away her tears, and continued to cradle her in his arms. For a moment it looked as if the weeping was done, but then all at once, she fell against him again and started a new chorus of sorrow. When she had no more power to weep, she simply buried her face in his cloak.

"My dear, I am an old man and if I sit in this position even one moment longer, I fear that my bones will become permanently fixed in this position." Josiah smiled at Hadassah as he said it, this time cradling her chin in his palms.

She sighed, really not wanting to leave his embrace, but also feeling a bit awkward by the body closeness of a man who was neither her near-kinsman nor her husband. As she pulled her moist cloak about her face and head, Josiah saw the embarrassment and wished again that he had not followed her.

"Do not be ashamed, please. I feel that you have honored me today with your tears."

This time Josiah sighed heavily to himself. He was always at a loss when it came to the emotions of women, but today he wanted so badly to hear from this woman all that she was thinking and feeling. Hadassah straightened her clothing, but tightened her cloak about her face even more. Josiah took note of the fact that it was a lovely face, but marked more by lines and dark shadows rather than age. He knew what his resurrection from the dead had cost in terms of a normal life; he wondered – based on the misery in her face - what Hadassah had paid.

"Why have you never married?" Josiah queried none too delicately, groaning sincerely because of the pain in his joints caused by sitting too long in one position.

As the older man kept trying to straighten his aching frame, while rubbing his knees and legs to increase circulation, Hadassah had time to consider what was in back of his question. This time, they both strolled along together silent for a few moments.

"I've never been asked," came the slow, quiet response. Unfortunate for Josiah, Hadassah was a woman of few words.

"How did you get away so quickly?" asked Hadassah, this time of him.

She had made it no further than two kilometers away from the catacombs when Josiah had been able to reach her. Josiah took note of Hadassah's strange habit of twisting the cloak tighter and tighter about her already covered face. This time he frowned at her.

"You wouldn't believe what happened when you were able to make your escape!" exclaimed the older man. "Someone in the crowd asked where you had gone, and said that they recognized you as one that the Master had also raised from the dead."

Josiah seemed amused in the remembering, but Hadassah was horrified. She stopped dead in her tracks and faced him squarely while peering all around for mourners who had perhaps indeed followed him to her.

"Not to worry, my dear Hadassah, no one followed me. They were focused on other things," he stated flatly.

Hadassah caught the odd change in his countenance and tone, but was distracted by the pain in her knee. She must have fallen directly on the jagged edge of the rock, and caused more damage than she had initially thought. She grimaced each time she took a step, and wished that she was able to remove her garment to give it a closer inspection. This was out of the question given the current circumstances, so she feigned tiredness so that she could shift her weight from it if only for a moment. Josiah, on his part, was glad for her slowed pace. Though agile for an elderly man, he had not run through his life as she had, nor walked too quickly either. He had long since accepted notoriety as part of his lot in life, and had learned even as a young man how to use it for its best advantage. A woman, on the other hand, he reflected, would certainly have had a tougher time of it.

The sun would soon be setting and Hadassah did not want to be on the roads alone, and that included her present company. She looked to Josiah who appeared deep in thought over something, and was willing now to disclose her anxieties.

"Josiah," she spoke his name to interrupt his daydreaming, "I believe I am hurt. When I stumbled at your call, a stone pierced my knee. I am also weary from the day's events, and had hoped to take refuge in the home of a family friend while in Bethany for the night." Josiah, who had honestly forgotten that she was even there, was startled momentarily by her pronouncement.

"My dear, of course," he replied. "Do you know the way? I too had made plans to stay with near kinsman, but this is not the direction of their home."

At this, Hadassah sighed heavily, and wished that she had not made this journey at all. In her efforts to get away, she had not stopped to consider which direction she was headed as she ran. She had in fact, run in the wrong direction. To turn back now, would mean that she might run into groups of the mourners who would, by custom, stay in Bethany for several days to mourn with the family of Lazarus.

"You said a woman at the tomb called out my name?" she looked at him with a heavy heart and was ready to follow his lead as long as it was not back towards the direction they had come.

"Yes," replied Josiah, "someone did recognize you. But it was not a woman – it was a man. I am trying to remember where I have seen him before. He of course recognized me as well. But that was not the main thing that happened. You asked how it was I got away," Josiah paused as he remembered something peculiar, "it was because of an assembly of disorderly Pharisees who came to the tomb demanding to see the body of Lazarus. They came wanting to see proof of his grave clothes. What an outrage and affront to our very laws and customs!"

This time the both of them stood staring at each other. Hadassah stared, trying to make sense of what significance grave clothes would hold. Josiah stood staring back at her, because he knew and had long since grown tired of describing the experience. She had never been buried in grave clothes, but both Josiah and Lazarus had.

CHAPTER TWO

Sound was not the first thing that was indelibly marked in Josiah's memory of coming back from the dead. In fact, he wished to God that his memory of coming back could have been a bit more pleasant than it was. Although later he would recall in vivid detail the sound of wailing, particularly that of his mother, it was the dreadful stench of his own rotting, decomposing tissue mixed with the scent of aloes and myrrh that he first remembered. All these years later, even the subtlest scent of certain herbs and spices made him sick to his stomach.

It was the Jewish custom of the day to prepare dead bodies very quickly for the burial because of the effect of the Palestinian hot climate on decomposing flesh. His corpse had been given a ceremonial washing for purification, and then strips of linen containing spices and herbs wrapped around his body to camouflage the smell. The body was then covered from head to foot with a burial shroud made of white linen. Because he was a man, and because his father was already dead, his mother had requested that the prayer shawl of his father be wrapped around his upper torso as well. As Josiah reflected on all of this perhaps a million times since his resurrection, it was the suffocating napkin tied about his head which blocked his airways that had first frightened him the most. Could one imagine waking up from the dead and not being able to breathe?

He could remember trying to say something, but above the din of the wailing and weeping, the sounds he was able to make were muffled by the head napkin which was wrapped too tightly around his windpipe. Every part of him, including his bones, was screaming. He thought the nerves and blood vessels in his muscles were being constricted by the linen strips filled with the pungent spices, but in actuality, the decomposition of the organs and tissues had been thrown into reverse. The prickly, stabbing pain caused by the ignition of bones, sinew, tendons and nerves was forever seared in his memory.

The burial shroud which covered the strips of spices made the entire experience even ten times worse. This one, not only felt heavy, but blocked any light from penetrating. One of his first thoughts was that he must have ended up in hell. The tight, desperate sensation caused by the feeling of asphyxiation and paralysis would haunt him for many days and cause bed sweats. Moreover, from that day until this, he had developed a terrible case of claustrophobia and could not tolerate the feeling of being hemmed in or encircled.

That is when he first heard that voice that was unlike the others. This one was not screeching and mournful. It was powerful, even demanding, and yet still and subdued. He heard it very distinctly say to him, "Young man, I know you can hear me. I want you to wake up! Arise!"

He felt the bier that they carried him on come to a complete stop, and even heard the protests of some who considered the approach of the Healer as an insult to the processional. He could feel his body begin to shake in convulsions as strong hands yanked the head napkin away from his throat and nasal passages. He could breathe! And, he could see light. It seemed like an eternity before his mind could adjust to what was happening around him. There was so much noise and tumult, that it took some time before he realized he was in fact the source of the chaos. There was mayhem directed against him from every direction, but the presence of the One who had spoken and thus saved his life seemed unmoved.

It was when the shroud was completely removed that he had plain vision of the Stranger's face. Josiah recognized Him immediately because of His fame throughout the region of Galilee and Judea. By Name, He was known as Jesus of Nazareth. More hands lifted the young man from the bier that had been lowered to the ground, and the Master held his gaze for many long moments. Josiah thought that he saw sadness there, but it would be many years into the future before he would reflect back and understand why.

His limbs kept buckling from under him as he tried to stand on brand new legs, and the terrible, close stench of his grave clothes mixed in with the sweet smell of myrrh in the heat caused him to faint. When he looked up again, he had fallen back to the bier that was now resting on the ground and the crowds of people reacted by pushing and shoving to see whether he was in fact dead or alive. The disciples of Jesus seemed to know what to do to bring order, and in an instant had cleared the space around the Master and Josiah, so that the widow of Nain could get to her son without injury. Simon Peter grabbed her in his arms just as she fainted as well. A few hours earlier, she had led the processional of her very dead and only son, headed to the tombs of Bethany. But now here he was standing on his feet and talking to her, "Mother, what is this all about? Why am I dressed as a dead man?"

Hadassah tried to bring Josiah back from his reverie, but knew from the experience of caring for her aging father that older people tended to take these excursions into their past as a matter of course.

"Josiah, please tell me. Why would the Pharisees demand to see the grave clothes of Lazarus? Why would they defile themselves by visiting a tomb?"demanded Hadassah.

When Josiah became aware that Hadassah was speaking to him and asking questions, he tried to hide his embarrassment by hailing a merchant for information. When the merchant paused hoping to make a sale, Josiah stepped up close to him and spoke something out of Hadassah's hearing. The merchant looked from one to the other of them with a nod of understanding and pointed eastward to the outskirts of the small village of Bethany. There were several small homes set into the hillside just beyond the slope of the road they all traveled on.

"There are several inns not far from my home, but it would be a blessing to me and my daughters if you would consent to lodge with us for tonight. I have no wife, but I do have two wonderful daughters, and you are welcome in my household until daybreak. My name is Eleazar of Bethany."

As Josiah peered at the merchant in cautious gratitude, he detected the faint smell of myrrh and frankincense and almost declined the offer. He knew, however, that it was too risky to go to an inn this evening. He could care less that people recognized him, as old as he was, but he felt responsible for the anxious state that Hadassah was in and thought better of his misgivings. She was still youthful enough to be easily recognized and there were, after all, more weighty things on which he needed her to focus her attention. Hadassah had stepped up beside Josiah because she wanted to be sure of the stranger for herself.

"I am Josiah of Nain. I am sure that you have heard many rumors of me."

It was said in such a dispassionate way, that initially Eleazar was not sure that he had heard his ears correctly. As he looked quickly from Josiah to Hadassah, his jaw dropped open in astonishment. Hadassah couldn't believe what Josiah had just done and restarted her obsession of twisting her cloak about her face.

"Sir," spoke the merchant in a reverent, hushed tone, "I too was healed by Jesus of Nazareth. You need not be afraid of reprisals from me and my daughters. You are among friends."

At this, Eleazar reached out to grasp Josiah by the shoulder in the typical gesture of brotherhood reserved to men. In turn, Josiah grasped his forearm and smiled with a nod. They both now looked to Hadassah for agreement, and Eleazar was able to reach out and grab her just before she fainted in his arms.

CHAPTER THREE

Someone was stroking her face with a soft linen cloth that had been dipped in scented water. The fragrance and the gentle touch of the hand lulled Hadassah back to consciousness. Hadassah looked up into the pretty face of a young woman about half of her age. The woman then turned quickly and called for her father Eleazar.

"Father, come quickly," the young woman cried, "her color has returned and she is awakened!"

Both Josiah and Eleazar bounded into the room like young boys and knelt down on the floor where Hadassah had been laid on a pallet. She reached up and grabbed the hand of Josiah who seemed flushed and greatly agitated. For a moment, her heart was saddened for him. How she wished that for once in her life she could give someone joy rather than pain. She had no way of knowing that the balance of her days would be spent doing just that.

"My daughter," Josiah said to her trying to hide the emotion in his voice, "is it well with you?"

She smiled up at him wordlessly. Eleazar took over from there.

"Hadassah, can you rise?" queried Eleazar.

She lifted up with the help of one of the women, and realized too late that she had no scarf with which to cover her face. All of them saw her agitation at once, and mistook it for pain.

"We will send for a physician at once…" started Eleazar, but then Hadassah was up and on the move before any of them could stop her.

"Oh no! Please! There is nothing wrong with me. I do not wish to be seen by a physician. Josiah, please…I do not wish to be seen…" her voice trailed off in despair, and for a moment, she thought of running into the night to escape the notoriety.

The women of the house rescued her before she could put the thought into action. The older of them, Dinah, performed the deft maneuver of getting both men out of the small enclave in less than thirty seconds. Tamar was the youngest woman and the one who had nursed Hadassah to health. When she saw Hadassah reach for her face, and remembered the old rumors about her, she quickly grabbed one of her own personal favorites, and wrapped it about Hadassah's shoulders.

"Hadassah, I am Tamar, and this is my sister Dinah. Welcome to our household!" exclaimed Tamar warmly.

She managed to clasp one of Hadassah's hands in her own, and bowed low before her to show deference. Dinah turned at her sister's introduction, and she too grasped Hadassah's forearm and squeezed it.

"Please," spoke Dinah with a smile as big as the heart it represented, "you must be hungry. It is just us here in the household. Do not be afraid, you are among friends."

Hadassah believed her and in spite of her fears, allowed herself to be cared for. As they all sat at a communal feast of salted fish, lentils, cucumbers, figs for dessert, and hot bread and wine, the two men kept vigil watching Hadassah for fear that she would faint again. Dinah and Tamar provided the dinner conversation with their chatter about the rumors circulating in the streets of Bethany concerning the happenings at the tomb of Lazarus. Hadassah was greatly surprised that she and Josiah were not after all the focus of the fresh rumors.

"Did they mention my name – did anyone say they saw me there at Lazarus' tomb?" Hadassah queried them in a rising level of anxiety.

The question surprised the two women, for though they knew her name and the fact that she had been raised from the dead, the news of her resurrection was old news in Bethany. It had been more than two decades since anyone had even mentioned her name. Dinah, being the oldest, heard that she'd died many years before. In fact, when her father brought both she and Josiah of Nain to their home that night, Dinah was more shocked to see that Hadassah was still alive than she was at the memory of the bizarre stories that used to abound about her visit to paradise. Although she had once seen Hadassah as a younger woman, her face was no longer familiar. Josiah was another matter, she mused to herself.

"My dear," Josiah spoke to her as gently as a father would his child daughter, "that is what I have been trying to tell you. When you were able to make your escape, a contingent of soldiers and a band of Pharisees created havoc at the tomb of Lazarus by demanding to examine his grave clothes."

Everyone at the table, including Eleazar, gasped.

"Although I stood there preparing to fight my way out of the crowd if need be, they soon forgot that I was even standing there," stated Josiah matter-of-factly.

At the remembering, even Josiah seemed utterly perturbed by the affront caused to the family of Lazarus. In Jewish society, the burial of the dead was considered a very sacred matter. Even the citizens of the dead person's village considered it a community obligation to ensure that certain decorum was followed with respect to their dead. A demand to examine the grave clothes was a clear violation. Josiah and Eleazar exchanged glances. It was clear that the men knew something that the women did not.

"Josiah, I need to know," Hadassah persisted. "You did not answer me earlier. Why would the Pharisees defile themselves by touching the grave clothes of the dead?"

The room grew quiet for a moment. And then in halting speech, Josiah shared with his new family the story of his resurrection from a casket made of perfumed linen cloths. When he was done, none was more stunned than Hadassah. She had been so consumed all of these years with her own private regrets of having been raised from the dead that she never considered that the events surrounding the resurrection of Lazarus and Josiah could have in any wise been worse than hers.

She couldn't imagine waking up from the dead to the smell of her own decomposing flesh clinging to grave clothes. They all just sat and stared at Josiah for a moment. He allowed it because he knew that it would relax Hadassah and keep the spotlight off of her as well. There was a request that he planned to make of her, and he knew that all of this would be needed to gain her trust of him. None of them queried him about the ghastly experience, but it was not out of respect for him, as much as it was out of respect for the One who had healed him. Josiah, of course, did not have this much needed perspective and neither did Hadassah.

"Did either of you ever become one of His disciples?" the question was asked by Eleazar, and initially it confused the two to whom he had directed it.

"I heard of His teachings many times from my father Jairus who greatly loved and respected Him," answered Hadassah.

"My daughter," responded Eleazar, "I knew your father long ago. Your father loved and respected the Master, and the Master loved your father as well."

This time Josiah spoke up after giving the question some thought. "I wished I had taken the opportunity to get to know Him better. I shall never forget His hand touch!"

Everyone in the room responded in unison with their own expression of wonder, agreement, and admiration. Hadassah was the only one, however, not fully persuaded that the hand had done her good. Then, Eleazar shared his own story.

"I was a young man of maybe eighteen or nineteen, not much older than you Hadassah when you were raised from the dead. I even remember hearing the reports about you, but until this day, never imagined that you were still alive. I'd also heard that you died not many years after you'd been raised from the dead."

Dinah and Tamar both nodded to affirm that they too were under the same understanding. Hadassah took the report in, careful not to show her bewilderment.

Died? She thought. *If everyone thought she was dead, then how did the woman...and later the man as reported by Josiah, recognize her at the tomb of Lazarus? How could it be that this merchant who was assaulted daily by rumors and news had heard that she was dead?!* Eleazar continued his story.

"I was stricken with leprosy during the time that my beloved Elisheba carried our third child, and soon after I was forced to go live in the catacombs, I lost both of them when the child, a son, was still-born," Eleazar swallowed hard at the memory, but it seemed to energize him rather than tire him.

"One day, there were ten of us on the road of a certain village. We heard that Jesus, the Healer of Nazareth would be passing by. Otherwise, we would never have ventured out in broad daylight, let me assure you! Someone brought the news that He would be passing that way, and we hid ourselves hoping that the report was true. We heard reports that He had the power to give sight to the blind, heal the lame and crippled, and loose the tongue of those who could not speak. We prayed diligently that He would also have pity on unclean lepers as well. There was one among us who was also a Samaritan, and initially we feared that the One from Nazareth might refuse to heal us because of him."

Eleazar looked around at the faces of his listeners, and began to weep without shame in front of the women gathered there. Dinah reached to give her father a cloth for his tears, but he waved her away.

"As the sun began to set on the day that He was appointed to come our way, we had all but given up hope of seeing Him. Some even came and laughed us to scorn as if there was something more that they could do to add to our wretchedness and hopelessness. They said that this Jesus of Nazareth would never agree to touch a Samaritan – they said He was a Rabbi, and that a Rabbi would never defile himself with a Samaritan. The logic of what they said made sense, and at first we thought to distance ourselves from our friend. I am ashamed today that the thought even crossed our minds. There we were, all of us unclean, and we considered turning our back on our brother."

Eleazar momentarily dropped his head in shame. The others sat quietly, not wanting to say anything that might insinuate a censure, for they all understood that to associate with a Samaritan was to some degree as bad as being a leper.

This time the tears of Eleazar flowed much freer, as he realized that those who sat with him on this occasion would neither judge him nor condone the offense to which he was now prepared to finally admit.

"The decision was made for us that evening, when at dusk, someone called to us that the Healer was coming our way. For fear that He would see the Samaritan and refuse to touch us, we hid ourselves and called out to Him from where we were, *Master, have mercy on us! Please, mercy...mercy!!*" As Eleazar described it, he raised his voice before his daughters and his guests and mimicked the actual way he and the other lepers had called out.

"He stopped for us and interrupted His journey to tell us to go show ourselves to the priest – that we were healed! We could scarcely believe it for each of us looked the same. We even felt the same, and for a moment doubted that it was true. We had heard that He needed to touch us to make us whole, and wondered if it had been a trick to get rid of us by the way."

Eleazar stopped again, this time to wipe his tears. Josiah noted that this reporting appeared to be good for Eleazar, for his face seemed to shine as he remembered.

"As we made our way to the priests in obedience to what the Master said to us, all at once, we each noticed the change in each of the others. The scabs and dark bruises disappeared, and where there had been dead skin and tissue, there was now clean, new flesh. We were clean! Can you imagine? We, who were filthy and abominable, were now clean... we could hardly believe it was so!" stammered Eleazar.

The memory which was now so vivid to him seemed to overwhelm him as he broke down and wept in his hands. Josiah motioned to his daughters to allow him this freedom and to not be ashamed of their father's tears. Josiah reached over and gave his friend the cloth for his tears, and this time it was accepted.

As Eleazar looked around the table, he swallowed hard, and Josiah could see that he needed to unburden himself of something he'd carried for too long. He just hoped that it would not affect their stay here tonight. He didn't know how or why, but somehow this man and his daughters, and this night was going to change his life forever. Sojourning with Hadassah after so many years, already had, but he also wanted whatever gift this man's testimony and home would bring.

Eleazar looked sorrowfully at his daughters and continued. "Once we saw that we were clean, we realized that we could not go to the priests in the company of a Samaritan."

He looked to Josiah with a plea in his eyes, and seemed to need the affirmation of another man at this point in his telling.

"I had a family to support..." he said pleading to Josiah, while looking back and forth at Dinah and Tamar. He sighed and continued once more.

"All of us realized that we had to go our separate ways and that meant denying any association with the Samaritan. We learned later that he alone went back to the Master to worship Him for giving all of us our lives back. You can't know how many times in all of these years since my healing that I wish I could turn back time and not care about what someone would have said or thought, and just worshipped at the Master's feet..."

Eleazar's voice trailed off into regret, and all of the others sat with him allowing him this time of repentance. And what a glorious repentance it was. All at once, he broke and wept and wept. The tears seemed to wash away something stored in his soul, and with full abandon, he clasped his hands before the others, and began to lift glory and praise to the Man from Galilee who had healed him so long ago.

His daughters sat weeping as well, for they had never understood the shadows in their father's face, and had always mistook it for prolonged grief over the premature death of their mother. They had only been partly right. Most of the grief had been borne of guilt. Now he was free in his soul. They knew it because his tears suddenly turned to laughter.

Josiah was astonished as he peered at Eleazar. Here was a man who had lived many years with the stench of decaying, decomposing flesh all around him in the catacombs of Jerusalem. He had never experienced the touch of the Master's hand, but had, with a cry for mercy, been freed from a dreaded disease by the same voice that had called him back from the dead as well. It also didn't escape Josiah's attention that Eleazar's life was now filled with the very fragrance that he himself abhorred.

Hadassah was astonished as well. As she peered at Eleazar, she thought of the many lepers she'd seen in her life. At their approach, even from afar, someone would yell, *Leper! Leper!* and everyone would run from them in great fear including young children. The unclean would then scurry away like wide-eyed and unearthly creatures, struggling to cover their faces with woolen, stained tunics. The stench of their open, festering sores and wounds, along with their unwashed bodies just added to the fear of them. Eleazar had spent a good part of his life running, hiding, tormented by the stares of unkind people, spat at and pummeled by rocks. *Eleazar,* she reflected, *had been brought back from the dead as much as she.* Hadassah marveled that here he sat thankful to have been given another chance among the living.

Dinah and Tamar were astonished because although they knew that their father had once been a leper, they had never heard him mention the friendship with a Samaritan. Now they understood plainly why he always opened his home to strangers, and scolded them when they spoke unkindly about Samaritans. They realized at that moment, that he had always been forgiven of his crime against his friend. No, what had just happened this night for their father was redemption. They smiled at each other, for they knew that he had won his freedom through the confession of a sin committed more against the Master than the Samaritan. This matter had bound him and haunted his conscience for many years following his healing.

Tamar looked at him and spoke the words that she'd heard the disciples of Jesus quote from the Master so many times, "If the Son therefore shall make you free, ye shall be free indeed." Tonight, Eleazar of Bethany had been made whole.

CHAPTER FOUR

While the Apostle Peter, once known as Simon Barjona, napped, an angel of the Lord revealed to him that Josiah of Nain and the daughter of Jairus had taken lodging for the night with Eleazar, one of the merchants of Bethany. He knew that because of the fresh rumors, that he must see them immediately. Earlier in the day, in the processional of the dead, he had been astonished to see both of them together at the tomb. Josiah still looked the same, but it was initially difficult to detect the woman because of her success in keeping her face covered. He sighed heavily. He was an old man now, and all of this intrigue made his bones ache.

"Father," came the gentle voice of one who served him, "what is it that troubles you tonight?" Peter looked up into the eyes of Eber and grabbed his arm.

"Eber, you must attend to a matter for me after the evening meal is done. Do you know the merchant Eleazar who lives at the edge of the village?" queried the aged apostle.

Eber nodded that he did.

"I can go now Father but I do not wish to leave you alone…you may need something more," replied the young man.

"No, my son Eber, you must go now before it gets too late. Let the others see to my needs here. Now go, it is important that I speak with the merchant Eleazar tonight. Please let him know that I must discuss an important matter with him tonight. He has one, Josiah of Nain, abiding in his home and I must address an urgent matter with this man right away."

Eber turned reluctantly to obey the command. He had served Peter since he was a young lad, and had learned so many things sitting at the feet of this wise man of God. He noticed more and more that the traveling was a great strain on him physically, and yet the apostle insisted on going anyway. This trip had been filled with so many surprises that Eber could hardly anticipate what strange thing might happen next. He would be glad when the burial of Lazarus was done.

A knock on the door to Eleazar's home startled everyone in the household as they talked and talked about the rumors that filled the little hamlet of Bethany this night. They each in turn had shared their thinking and concerns about the activities of the Pharisees at the tomb of Lazarus, and it was clear that nobody was in the mood for sleeping. Hadassah had become a different woman in a matter of a few hours. She was in the fellowship of other women and men who did not care a whit about her trip to paradise. She fussed with the serving pots, jars and communal dishes as is the custom of women to make sure that everything is just so, and there was lightness in her step and heart that had not been there in many years. She seemed relieved of some burden, and although she still took care to cover her face, deliverance had already begun in her soul. Before the night was over, she too would be made whole.

Eleazar was watching Josiah as he watched Hadassah when the knock came at the door. Surprised by the sudden interruption, they each froze, peering from one to another and then finally to the head of the house. Eleazar looked to his daughters for an explanation, but they each returned a bewildered look to him. No one was expected in their home tonight, not even present company.

"Father," spoke Dinah first, "the city is full of travelers tonight who have come to pay homage to Lazarus. It is probably someone seeking shelter."

Eleazar nodded at her suggestion and quickly arose to answer the door. He stepped out into the night to address the stranger, leaving everyone else in suspense. Their talk had put everyone on edge in a good way, but each of them privately discerned that the knock at the door would not be that of a stranger seeking refuge.

"Are you Eleazar, the merchant?" asked the young man of the elder.

"Yes, I am Eleazar. Why do you seek me?" responded Eleazar with caution.

"I am servant to one of the disciples of Jesus of Nazareth," replied Eber. "He has come to pay homage to Lazarus and has taken lodging tonight with Reuel the Potter. He requests an audience with both you and one of the visitors in your home tonight. He says that it is urgent and will not wait until the morning light."

Eleazar stared at the young man, momentarily unable to speak.

"Yes, my son, I will come, but what does he want of me?" he probed. Eber bowed out of respect and repeated himself, "He says that the matter is urgent and will not wait until morning. He desires an audience with the both of you. He awaits our return."

Josiah was burning with curiosity from inside of the house and could wait no longer for a return by Eleazar. He too stepped out into the night to stand beside Eleazar.

"What is it Eleazar? Is there some matter of which I may be assistance?" inquired Josiah of both men.

Eleazar turned to him and introduced the young man as a servant of one of the disciples of Jesus of Nazareth. As yet, he had not asked which one. Eber, who was more astute than most imagined, was momentarily stunned when he looked into the face of Josiah. Although he had heard of the miracle of this man's resurrection from the dead too many times to count, there was something about actually standing in his presence that evoked awe. Eleazar repeated the request of the Apostle hastily to Josiah, as the thoughts in his mind raced trying to make sense of how anyone would have known that Josiah and Hadassah had taken lodging in his home that night. They had not met anyone on the road as they came, and because Hadassah was in such a state with blood on her outer tunic, both men had been anxious to get her to his home.

"Eber, although I respect this disciple of the Master highly, I cannot consent to this request tonight," started Josiah.

Eleazar stared at him puzzled. Yes, it was late, but any disciple of Jesus would be considered a celebrity in Bethany. In Eleazar's estimation, the denial of such a small request seemed insulting.

"Please take him word that we will agree to speak with him in the morning," Josiah continued, "but tonight we must take rest. I do not wish to overtax this man or his household further," Josiah stated coldly.

Thinking that this would end the matter altogether, Josiah turned abruptly and retreated back into the home of Eleazar. He meant no disrespect to an apostle of Jesus, but his own life of notoriety had taught him that there were few things in life that could not wait until a better time. When he was younger, people would often send word to him insisting upon an immediate audience. He learned early on that the urgency they claimed was rarely legitimate, and that if he lived his life at the whims of people's curiosity, he would never have a life at all.

Of course, Eleazar's perspective was different. Not only had he been graced that night to provide lodging to two of the most well-known celebrities in the region, but now here he was being bidden to the presence of a living disciple of Jesus. When Josiah turned to leave, Eleazar turned to Eber and whispered something in his ear. Eber turned quickly to leave, but was greatly agitated that he had not performed what was requested of him.

The turn of events now added something new to the atmosphere in the home that was already charged with tension. Neither of the men, however, seemed willing to share it with the women. They remained tight-lipped about the matter at the door until a second knock came less than an hour later. There would be no sleep in this house tonight.

At the second knock, Eleazar locked eyes with Josiah. They both thought the same thing at the same time, but they were wrong.

"Father, do you wish me to answer?" asked Dinah.

"Of course not!" replied Eleazar who was genuinely offended that his daughter would think of answering a knock at the door in the night with men present in the household.

Neither he nor Josiah was a spring chicken, but they weren't mutts either. Both of them had bad backs, but between the two of them they had one good one. "We will answer," he turned to Josiah and nodded at him, signaling for him to join him outside. He assumed that the young man had returned with a new message from the Apostle. He would not be the one to refuse any request made by a disciple of Jesus. No, Josiah would have to answer for himself.

When they swung the door open, it was Eleazar who fell back first and gasped at the presence of a man who himself had raised the dead. It was the Apostle Peter of Bethsaida, who now made his home in Jerusalem. There was an anointing all about the aged disciple of Jesus that was so electric, that one had to fight off the urge to fall prostrate at his feet. Eleazar started to do just that, when the apostle discerned his intent and stopped him with a wave of his hand. He stood leaning on a wooden walking stick in one hand, with a heavy outer mantle wrapped about him against the chill of the night.

Josiah stood staring at him, trying to remember where he knew him so well. He realized that this was the Apostle Peter who stood before him; but, he kept searching the face of the Apostle because there was something familiar about him that he could not place. At the tomb of Lazarus he had not recognized him as the Apostle, but as he stood here now, he remembered that this was the man who had walked up to him and asked about Hadassah's well-being. Still, he was nagged by the sense that he knew this man from somewhere else.

"I was the one who caught your mother when she fainted during your funeral procession," answered Peter matter-of-factly.

This time, Josiah was the one who fell back stunned by the revelation.

"Yes! I remember you now. I almost choked from the head napkin which was wrapped about my throat, and you were one of those who removed it so that I could breathe," exclaimed Josiah.

Josiah stood remembering out loud, and it was Eleazar who finally broke his trance so that they could get the aged statesman inside to warmth and hospitality.

"Please, come in! Come inside!" insisted Eleazar.

He was nearly overcome with emotion. Peter had ministered healing and deliverance to the blind, the lame, the brokenhearted, and to lepers throughout the regions of Galilee as well as Judea. One of his best friends, Clopas of Bethany, had been mightily healed by the Apostle Peter. He smiled thinking of Clopas who never tired of telling the story of how he had laid at the Gate Beautiful at the Temple for so many years begging alms and how Peter and John healed him with the words, "Silver and gold, have I none, but such as I have, in the Name of Jesus of Nazareth, rise up and walk." Clopas, ironically, lived no more than a stone's throw from his home. He had not seen the Apostle Peter again after his miracle of healing and spoke so many times of his desire to see him once more before he died. Secretly, Eleazar began to plot how he could get word to Clopas, who had been born lame from his mother's womb, that the man whom God had used to heal him was in his home that very night.

They could hardly get the Apostle settled comfortably because of the women, including Hadassah, who rushed about getting this and doing that to wash his feet, warm his hands, and to get him seated comfortably on a low stool. Finally, Peter motioned for Eber to please make them stop.

"Father, they love you and want to honor you. You deserve the attention," responded the young man over Peter's objections.

"No! Please...All of you...I have come tonight for important business. I am honored to be in your house tonight Eleazar. May the peace of our Lord and Savior, Jesus Christ, and the sweet communion of his Holy Spirit, be upon you and your household this night. While the Master sojourned with us, He taught us that whenever we entered a home that received us in the name of a prophet, to let our peace be upon that household. And it is so, my dear brother Eleazar!" cried the Apostle who was the only natural man who ever lived who had walked on water.

Eleazar sat before him and wept unashamed. On later reflection, he would look back to this night and marvel at the power of ordinary events to shift a life. Peter peered back and forth at each of them, and then his eyes settled on Hadassah.

"Hadassah," he spoke her name softly, "I remember you so well. You were a girl of only twelve when the Master called you back from the dead. Is it well with you?" Peter queried.

"Yes Sir, it is well with me," Hadassah lied.

Peter knew it, but decided to overlook it for the moment.

"And Josiah, I shall never forget the day of your resurrection... you were nearly trampled to death again by the mourners. Is it well with you?" asked Peter with a twinkle in his eye.

They thought the Apostle was making small talk, but he wasn't.

"It is well with me, and I hope with you as well," responded Josiah.

Although both he and Hadassah were equally honored by the presence of so great a guest as Peter, they were unmoved by the sentiment.

"We have heard the rumors in Bethany about Lazarus," interrupted Josiah, "we are surprised to see you here. You are not one to frequent tombs or wail for the dead."

Peter did not look at Josiah when he spoke, but rather kept his attention focused on Hadassah. His attention opened up old wounds for her and before she knew it, she was twisting the scarf of Tamar around her face again.

"Hadassah," Peter spoke her name firmly but softly, "when our Lord called you back from the dead, you got caught between two worlds – that of the living and that of the dead."

Hadassah stared at him and without realizing it, dropped the scarf and momentarily buried her face in her hands. *How many times had she commiserated over the fact that she felt caught between two worlds?*

"It would have been easy for your father and your mother to let you die that day once they got the report that all hope was lost, but they knew that the gift of God is life – life eternal. I remember it so clearly…like it was just yesterday…." The Apostle's voice trailed off momentarily.

He seemed lost in thought as he recalled the incident of Hadassah's death back to his memory.

"You were not dead yet when your father was able to fight his way through the crowds that surrounded us. When he left you with your mother, you were still alive."

Peter seemed tired, but it was as if something else weighed on his heart and mind. He sighed heavily and continued.

"I am an old man and I have seen many things, but I have never met any man who loved his little daughter as much as Jairus loved you. By the time he got to us, he was half dead himself. He looked like he had cried all the way, and his feet were bloody from blisters."

Peter shook his head as he remembered the state that Jairus was in when he arrived, and the memory made him close his eyes as if he was seeing the arrival of Jairus right there in front of him.

"When he managed to get to our Lord, he fell exhausted and weeping at the feet of the Master and buried his face in the hem of the robe of our Lord – along with about fifty others who were clinging as well!" continued Peter.

Hadassah sat staring at the rabbi in wonder. Her father had always started the report of her resurrection at the moment when Jesus had put everyone out of her room before He called her back from the dead. Her father had never told her this part of the story, and her mother would not have known to tell it for she would not have witnessed it.

Peter continued. "When he fell at the Master's feet, he was so overcome that he could hardly speak. He kept clutching his chest as he tried to get the words out. He bargained with the Lord to take his life rather than yours and to please come and heal his little girl who was home gravely ill, at the point of death."

As Peter spoke, he kept his eyes fastened on Hadassah; he knew that he was pouring oil and wine into an open, festering wound that had robbed her life of laughter and promise.

"Your father, Jairus, promised our Lord that for the balance of his days that he would forever give God the glory."

Josiah took quiet notice of the fact that Hadassah was no longer hiding her face, and he marveled that the lines about her eyes seemed to vanish. Even in his advanced age, there were still stories that the Apostle effected cures and miracles. Could it be, wondered Josiah, that he was working a real-life miracle right there before them? Eyes and limbs were easier to detect for transformation, but a conversion took discernment.

"Hadassah," the Apostle called her name now in a hushed, stern tone, "you are not the only one who was dying that day. Jairus was not the only father there that day who sought our Lord for a miracle. Your mother was not the only one that day whose heart hoped against hope. There were many, Hadassah, I tell you multitudes and multitudes kept coming and coming from every direction and with every form of filthy, mean sickness and disease you can imagine. Many were bound by unclean spirits and demons that would run to the Master tearing their hair out, foaming at the mouth, biting and cursing. The whole lot of them smelled to high heaven!" The Apostle's vivid accounting held the small group before him spell-bound.

"On that particular day that Jairus came to us desperate and pleading, there were so many people for whom the Master had already prayed, that we begged the Master to stop and take rest. We reminded Him that He could not possibly answer every plea, heal every diseased person or run to every difficult case there on the hillside that day. You are not alive today because you were the only one dying that day! There were so many pushing and shoving to get to Him that some grew belligerent and even accosted Him. One woman who had suffered a twelve year issue of blood and had suffered many things at the hands of a number of physicians, crawled through dirt, rocks, profanities, and insults trying to touch just the hem of His garment in hopes that this would bring healing."

The Apostle halted to let the significance of his words sink in past Hadassah's pain.

"You are alive because the Savior of the world made a choice to step over the needs of others to get to you, then, only a little girl. He made a path that day through a mass of people who were defiled, infected and infirmed to reach you that day. Had we had our way, believe me, you would have stayed dead that day, and your father would have gone home a tormented and broken man." The Apostle paused so that the full effect of his words could sink in.

"There are many called, Hadassah, but only a few are chosen. Our Lord chose you that day because of the great purpose on your life. It was not your father's words or tears that made you our Lord's choice. When your members were yet unformed in your mother's womb, our God knew you and chose you – even before the foundation of the world, He chose you."

Everyone in the room was beginning to see the powerful truth of Peter's words, and there was not a dry eye among them, save Josiah.

"You have spent your life between the world of the living and the world of the dead, and have not once stopped to consider that God is God of both the living and the dead. In all places and in all things, He is the Eternal God. If you had died as a young girl, you would have died unto Him. Instead, He chose you so that you might live unto Him. But you have done neither. If it is true, as you have said, that you had been better off dead than alive, then when you stand in the resurrection and you must give an account of your life, what will the heavens declare of your death? If, as you have said, your life has been worth nothing, then tell me, what would your death have been worth?"

The Apostle peered at her as if he actually wanted an answer. She covered her face with her hands and ran from the room in tears. Peter held up his hand to all present to indicate that they were not to follow her to comfort her.

He turned to all of them now as a group and spoke, "the day will come when every man will stand before our God and give an accounting of the deeds done in this flesh. And at that great day, each must stand alone. Do not grieve for Hadassah, for once again, our Lord has offered her another chance to live. It is time for her to make the decision to cast aside the grave clothes with which she hides her face."

At this, the Apostle Peter dropped his head in reflection; not because he was sad or sorry, but because he realized that as he spoke the words, that they were for him as much as for these who heard them. It would be some time after the night's twists and turns before Josiah would really hear the words with his heart, but when he did, he too would be a changed man forever.

When Hadassah fled, she fled to the rooftop of the home of Eleazar. There, she felt great chains of oppression and depression crush under the anointing of the man of God. There was something happening in her spirit that made her shake from head to foot. The trembling seemed to move from the inside out. As she stretched prostrate before the open heavens, she did something she had never done before in her life. She prayed for herself. She repented of the anger that she had secretly harbored against God for sending her back from the dead. She repented for the anger she felt at her mother for the hurtful words she had spoken. She repented for loving and hating her father all at the same time and for the prison she had allowed him to build about her life with his fabrications. She repented for self-loathing and for hating the day she was born. She repented for building a sepulcher in her own soul.

On the street below, someone was listening to her testimony, although she did not know it then. It was Clopas, the man whom Peter and John had healed at the Gate called Beautiful. He had spent most of the evening at the home of Lazarus, and had now to be guided back home in the dark by a household servant. He was an old man now and felt tired of life, and had come to dread these macabre productions for the dead. He turned and looked upwards toward the sound of singing and worship coming from the roof of Eleazar, and wondered why Tamar or Dinah would be up on the roof at this hour singing so loudly. His body ached, but his spirit was hungry for something more.

He signaled for his manservant to help him cross the small thoroughfare that led to the outer walls of Eleazar's home. Although he had had enough talk for one night, he decided that it would only take a moment to stop and exchange information with his good friend Eleazar, the merchant who always had a good story to tell. As he headed toward the home of his friend, he wondered if there could be any truth to the strange rumors about the grave clothes of Lazarus. He was eager to get Eleazar's point of view on the whole matter.

CHAPTER FIVE

Josiah could not help but be worried about Hadassah. He secretly felt that the Apostle had been a bit too strong. Everything he said certainly sounded like it had merit, but how could anyone who had not gone through what they'd been through know what it felt like to be hounded and ogled everywhere you went?

It wasn't that they weren't grateful for being brought back from the dead, he thought to himself, *it was the fact that they couldn't live out their lives in peace!*

He was startled suddenly when he looked up to see the Apostle focused on him as if he could read his thoughts.

No, don't be fooled, Josiah! Keep your wits about you and just meet him eye to eye. He can't read anybody's mind. He is just staring at you because he thinks he has the right to judge those who are not as spiritual as he.

The women were talking once again about the rumors regarding Lazarus, but Josiah squirmed under the fixed gaze of the Apostle. It bothered him the more when he noticed that it was not anger or offense that he saw in the eagle eyes of Peter – but rather, something shrewd and perceptive.

Just as suddenly, the Apostle turned from Josiah and joined the discussion about Lazarus.

"Josiah was correct when he observed that I am not a man who frequents catacombs and processionals of the dead. The Master taught us that the dead should bury the dead."

The Apostle spoke it dispassionately, although for Josiah it stung because of the private matter he had been hiding from Hadassah.

"I am here," continued Peter, "because of a rumor that started with the disciples and has persisted about Lazarus throughout his life. I was there on the day that the rumor first took root. It involved a conversation I had with the Master concerning Lazarus that was overheard and repeated by others who added something that the Master never said. The first error was thus made worse by the second error. But before I share the rumor, it is important that you first hear the full story of the miracle of Lazarus' resurrection from the dead. Would one of you please go and bring Hadassah down from the rooftop...it is important for her to hear this as well. Josiah, since you've made Hadassah a key figure in your scheme, why don't you go and fetch her. When you finally tell her what you have planned for her, the information she is about to hear will help her put the things you are planning in proper perspective."

For quite a few moments, Josiah did not move. He was stunned and then he was afraid. For one thing, he realized that the Apostle was no ordinary man for he had read the motives of his heart as clearly as if he'd spoken his plans out loud. Secondly, while it was true that he had plans for Hadassah that were not necessarily pure, he did not want to be misunderstood or judged for what he felt would benefit them both. Third, and this one was the most worrisome of all, he did not want the Apostle to expose his hand too quickly. There were other things that needed to be put in place first so that Hadassah would not balk at the peculiar nature of the idea.

All of the others now sat staring at Josiah, and Eleazar reflected to himself that he had sensed something all along. There had been something in the manner of Josiah that he found deeply troubling, although he could never have imagined the devices he had up his sleeve. *This Peter*, thought Eleazar, *was nobody to toy with – even as an old man.* He'd once heard the story that a husband and wife had dropped dead at his feet for trying to hide something from him, although he did not know how true the story really was. He wondered, with amusement, if Josiah had ever heard the story.

As Josiah rose slowly, using his age to hide his contemplation, a sudden knock at the door surprised everyone including Peter. The daughters of Eleazar looked this time at their father in amusement, for theirs was a quiet household of habitual custom and rituals. They couldn't remember ever experiencing a night like this one before, but they were enjoying every moment of it – and now they were about to hear the story of how Jesus had raised Lazarus from the dead by a man who was a living eyewitness to the most infamous event in Bethany.

When Eleazar swung the door of his home open for the third time that night, he was greatly unsettled to stand there looking into the half-concealed faces of Mary and Martha, the sisters of Lazarus. Right behind them, and bringing up the rear, was his good friend Clopas who had on so many occasions talked about how much he longed to see the Apostle Peter just one more time before he left this earth. *What a night, what a night*! mused Eleazar to himself.

CHAPTER SIX

Josiah interrupted Hadassah's worship to bring her back down to the main story of the house at the Apostle Peter's request. He had stayed long enough to see that the new guests to arrive were none other than the sisters of Lazarus in their mourning garments. While it was true that he had desired an audience with them before he left Bethany, he did not want to meet them under the present circumstances.

As he steadied Hadassah on her feet and checked her to make sure that she truly looked okay, the smell of flower petals, herbs and stems, and seeds from a variety of plants almost caused him to heave with nausea. He peered around the rooftop at a number of objects stored there which were used for the preparation of perfumes and ointment, along with a large press which women used to wring oil from crushed flowers. He started gagging as the aroma of nard and other fragrances filled his lungs. His eyes and throat burned from the assault and all at once he started sneezing and wheezing. He turned too quickly to escape the torture chamber he found himself in, and stumbled over the wooden frame of the bag press used to crush flowers for oil.

When he fell, the sound of his tumble made a thundering clatter which could be heard by the guests below. Hadassah scrambled to help him up as best she could, while still trying to come back to earth from her wondrous worship. She felt like a mightily changed woman, although instinctively she reached for her scarf once she was able to get Josiah to his feet. What a sight the two of them were together. Hadassah was trying to regain her balance and clear her head, while Josiah's nose and eyes ran water. When they finally got each other down the stairs safely and entered the main room of the house used for family meals, they were taken aback to find everyone seated and quiet as if waiting for their arrival. Momentarily, both of them stood staring at the room full of guests, and it was Mary who broke the ice with a smile and greeting for Josiah.

"Josiah is it well with you?" she asked in a pained effort to sound charitable.

"I was, when the evening started at your house, my dear," Josiah said it with a smile in his voice.

He could see that both of the sisters of Lazarus looked fatigued and utterly cheerless. Why on earth would they leave the multitude of guests and friends gathered at their home to venture out tonight...and for what important purpose? Martha seemed to read his thoughts and stood to give space for the older man to sit in her place.

"There is an urgent matter that we needed to discuss with the Apostle Peter," stated Martha, "and we were told by someone who passed him on the road as he traveled here, that it was the home of Eleazar where he had taken lodging for the night."

Now everyone turned to look at Peter, who had been sitting there the entire time with his eyes closed and his head down – almost as if he were in prayer.

"Father," Eber spoke the endearment softly, "is it well with you?"

The Apostle who had once seen Jesus feed 5,000 people with a few fishes and loaves looked around the room to those who were assembled there and gave them a gentle nod. Clopas could hardly contain himself.

"Apostle... do you remember me?"cried Clopas.

He had moved swiftly from where he was seated opposite Eleazar and had managed to get to the feet of Peter before Eber could block him. Peter raised his hand to stop Eber, but also looked at him with a knowing smile. He as well as the other disciples used to do the same thing when people, even children, tried to disturb Jesus. He even laughed to himself at the absurdity of the thought now that he was aged and more mature in his thinking. The Master always saw in them their future as apostles, but they never once really understood any of it until long after His death and resurrection. They saw their chief responsibility to Him to act as His body guards to keep sick people, blind people, women, and small children away. *How thoughtless we were as disciples*, thought Peter to himself. Although in many ways they had come to understand the mission of the Lord, they had entirely missed His vision.

Clopas brought the Apostle out of his reverie, by burying his face in the cloak of Peter as he knelt at his feet. The two of them were very close in age, and the feat was not nearly as easy for Clopas as it appeared.

"Clopas," Peter called to him while signaling for him to rise, "I am a man such as you, please, please, arise."

Peter could see that he was weeping and asked the same question of him that he had earlier asked of Josiah and Hadassah.

"Tell me, Clopas, what have you done with your life?" asked Peter.

Momentarily, the question stunned the man who had once begged alms for a living. He was speechless. After receiving his miraculous new chance at life, his whole world seemed to have turned upside down. He was not about to admit it, but he had actually done very little.

"I…I am an old man, Rabbi, and I am afraid there is not much that these old bones are good for," Clopas stammered.

He was fumbling with his tunic and peering all about now, hoping that someone would rescue him from the undue attention.

"Sit," was the quiet command from Peter.

Clopas nodded his head in embarrassment, but also submission and returned to his seat next to the family hearth.

"Clopas," Peter called to him once he had settled himself on a pallet next to the fireplace, "have you ever stopped to consider why you were singled out for the miracle of healing to your limbs?"

At first, the tears of Clopas had been for sentimental reasons at seeing the man who had raised him from a life of helpless dependence, but now the tears flowed from conviction. Quite frankly, he had never considered his miracle as having any other purpose, other than the wonderful fact that he could walk on limbs that were not fully formed and misshapen.

This time they all looked and listened with great interest, for there was something about the eyes and the manner of the man of God which had a divine quality to it. There were times when the Apostle would lift his eyes toward something in the air and peer at it as one who could see the invisible. At other times, his eyes would circle the room, and rest momentarily and fixed on just one person as he spoke to the whole group. Each waited eagerly, including the sisters of

Lazarus, to hear what he might have to say about the assortment of rumors flying about, but Peter had more than that in mind.

"Perhaps the most troubling thing I ever saw the Master deal with, were people who had been abused by demonic spirits. Once their minds and bodies were free of these unclean spirits, I always wondered what became of them. Although there were some who left everything they had to follow the Master after their miracle, most did not, and as disciples we never knew what became of their lives."

Peter paused to look at the group before him. He could feel the tension in the air, and was not interested in playing games with them, but was also greatly discomfited by the assortment of private agendas around him. He sighed deeply and began the story that all of them longed to hear.

"We were just south of Judea when the Master received word that Lazarus was sick unto death," began Peter as he looked now upon the faces of Mary and Martha.

The two women peered back at him, eager to hear. They were both also advanced in their years, and Peter took note of the fact that it was many a time when these two women had blessed the Savior as well as the twelve with their hospitality and thoughtfulness. He prayed silently that before his death God would allow him some small thing to do for them that would truly bless their lives.

"We were tired and also in great distress over the reports that the Pharisees were plotting to kill the Master. These reports came to us daily, but the Master seemed unmoved by them. We were consumed by our own private fears that we could be killed as well. And what had He done to deserve their hatred and their plotting?" the Apostle spread his hands before them. "He had hurt no one, stole from no one, broken no law, and yet they sought openly to take Him by stealth and take His life!"

The Apostle shook his head as he remembered, and sighed heavily as the memories crowded now into his mind's eye. He actually did not enjoy the telling of these stories so closely tied to the events of the Last Supper with the twelve, for inevitably, he had to remember his denials as well.

"On our part, we all had just seen Lazarus not many weeks before. He seemed fine to us then, and we knew that whatever was wrong with him, that the two of you would see him up, about, and fully cared for in short order," Peter said to Mary and Martha.

"In our minds, there was no cause for alarm at this report, but of course the Master knew all along just how bad things had gotten with him. We knew how much the Master loved him. We knew that if things were as bad as the two of you were reporting that the Master would not hesitate to go to him. In fact, it never occurred to us that we would return to Judea at all. So it was not just the fact that the Master did not react to your call for Him to come, it was that we knew that we could not return to Judea at all."

"Peter," Martha spoke it softly to a man whom she had come to love greatly and respect even more, "We too had heard the talk that the Pharisees planned to take Jesus and kill Him, and when you did not come speedily, we thought that it was because of the threats. As oft as the Savior sat at meat in my house, you would think I would have known Him better. Threats never bothered Him."

Both Mary and Martha exchanged looks with each other and nodded silently. When the Master delayed in coming to Lazarus, it wasn't just the two of them who commiserated about the delay of the Master – Lazarus did as well. In fact, Lazarus died feeling that the Savior had forsaken him in the hour that He could have once and for all proven His deity to him.

Peter waited for Martha to reflect for a moment and then continued. The episode of Lazarus' resurrection was a memory that brought back joy as well as great sadness, and many, many regrets by everyone concerned.

"Perhaps the biggest mistake we made as His followers is that we were always judging His actions by human standards. We were quite unable to understand that when He spoke, it was from two different dimensions – the spiritual as well as the natural. And He would speak from both dimensions at the same time. Since we did not recognize this about Him, we would only hear from the natural, but He would speak from the spiritual as well, and we typically missed His point about things wholly and completely," explained Peter.

"Sometimes I marvel that He tolerated us at all," continued Peter. "If He said up, we thought He meant the sky; if He said down, we thought He meant the ground."

Peter said this with a heavy sigh. It often burdened his heart greatly when he remembered what a rebel he had been, and he privately wished that he could go back and change so many things. Just earlier in the day, at the tomb of Lazarus, he ran into the son of the soldier whose ear he cut off in the Garden of Gethsemane. The young man recognized him at once and wanted to fall at his feet in honor. Peter wouldn't allow it because although his father had been changed after the Master put the ear back into place, the incident reminded him too much of how they had forsaken the Lord in His hour of soul anguish.

Mary saw the Apostle caught in the labyrinth of a memory, and interjected a memory of her own about Lazarus.

"You know, not many people know why Jesus loved him so," she began. "The two of them were as brothers – they had known each other most of their lives. It was the reason why Lazarus was so slow to believe that He was the Christ."

This time Mary was the one who sighed heavily, as she added, "familiarity can blind you to what is staring you in the face. Our fathers knew each other by trade as carpenters, and both Lazarus and Jesus first came to know each other as young boys learning the trade of our fathers. Work is always plentiful for a carpenter, and because the towns of our births were so close, it was often that we visited in the house of Joseph with Jesus and his sisters and brothers, and the same was true when they came to visit with us." Martha too smiled at the memory of the two families often uniting for the Sabbath observance.

"You know," offered Peter as he listened to the contributions of the sisters with a smile, "it not only got in his way of believing, but it always got him into hot water with the Master. Sometimes," Peter laughed, "more than me."

Both Mary and Martha chuckled together at this one, for Lazarus was always in trouble even with their father, because he insisted on seeing proof in everything.

Peter continued, "it is interesting that you mention his early days with Jesus, because although he tagged along with us, he never believed what he witnessed with his own eyes. It was as if seeing was not enough to believe, and I remember that the Master appeared privately pained about it. We never understood why he tolerated Lazarus around us, because He never allowed people who doubted to stay in His presence for too long. He taught us that doubt is as powerful as faith. He once said to us, 'As a man thinketh, so is he.' But He made Lazarus the exception. It was as if He knew and fully expected that one day Lazarus would come around. None of us could have ever suspected that he would come around from the dead!"

The women of Eleazar's house moved slowly about the assembly serving hot bread and wine, as well as an assortment of nuts, pomegranates, figs and melons. They felt like they were in heaven. Eleazar too was filled with great joy. This gift of having such a congregation as this in his home was more than he could have ever hoped for. He would never be the same again, and he knew that his home would never be the same again either. He looked quickly to Clopas who was seated to his left near the hearth. He knew that the Apostle was not finished with him yet, and hoped that the evening's events would somehow change his life as well.

"I remember," said Martha, "when Lazarus came home one day and shared with us the story of the day that they had gone into a certain town close to the Jordan to get meat for the Master, and found Him talking to a woman of Samaria at a well."

Peter looked at her and chuckled. He had been there, and he remembered the reaction of Lazarus well, because they all were outraged to find the Master talking to a Samaritan. The difference was that they were accustomed to the Master breaking the rules of their traditions, while Lazarus was not. He noted that Lazarus was a man who followed Jesus afar off.

Martha continued her interjection. "Most of the men in the regions of Judea as well as Galilee knew of her, and Lazarus could not believe that the Master would allow such a one to even stand in His presence, never mind the fact that she was a Samaritan. He seemed," Martha paused to say the next point, "to have lost a great deal of confidence in our Lord at this incident. He just could not believe that the Master would not see the wrong in mixing with Samaritans. Lazarus once told me after his resurrection, that he wished he could go back to that very well and leave the water pots of his life on the wall of that well, just as that Samaritan woman had done that day."

"Yes," continued Peter, "there were many things that our Lord did and even said that deeply troubled Lazarus, and each thing seemed to drive his doubt deeper. I remember once when our Lord said to us that if we were not willing to eat His flesh and drink His blood that we would have no part in Him. After these words, many turned back from following Him, and I noticed that Lazarus was greatly changed after these words, and seemed somehow less committed."

Martha interjected for fear that her brother's devotion to the Lord would be doubted because of these words, "but Peter, he still loved the Master so."

Peter peered at her understanding her intentions, but he was not one to capitulate merely for the purpose of sparing someone's feelings. The Apostle continued because he needed to expose a plot that was brewing in Bethany, and he knew that there were key people in that very room who were directly responsible for its potency. He would not allow any sentiment to distract him from his purpose in coming out that night, for he knew how high the stakes would get.

CHAPTER SEVEN

Josiah kept trying to hide his agitation at this unexpected twist in his trip to the burial of Lazarus. It seemed that his whole plan was coming loose at the seams, and it occurred to him that the three women whose help he needed most might make their decision against him based solely on what they were hearing here tonight. The Apostle had spoken prophetically when he sent Josiah to the rooftop to get Hadassah, and Josiah could see that indeed this journey down memory lane by the sisters of Lazarus and the Apostle Peter were having quite an effect on Hadassah.

At each new contribution to the story of Lazarus, he noticed that she seemed startled as if the new information she was hearing that night was solving some riddle in her head. This bothered him greatly, for though they both had listened to Dinah and Tamar share their versions of the rumors circulating about Lazarus, he couldn't remember now if Hadassah had really shared with him and the others what she had heard. What she had done, incessantly, was ask a lot of questions on his mention of the Pharisees and their demand to see the grave clothes of Lazarus. *What could she be thinking about all of this,* wondered Josiah, *and what was she thinking now that she knew that Lazarus and Jesus had been boyhood friends?*

Peter continued talking, but peered at Josiah, as if he had just heard his thoughts.

"After the two of you sent word that your brother was gravely ill and that you feared the worse, we thought no more of it when the Master told us that we were going to stay where we were a couple more days. In fact, the Master said to us that the sickness was not unto death, but unto God's glory. Well, we certainly never imagined that He purposefully allowed your brother to die so that it would result to God's glory!" Peter was talking directly to the two sisters now, though, much of it after all of these years, they still just didn't understand.

As Mary sat hanging on to each word of the Apostle, she couldn't help remember some things as well. She remembered how the people in their village were so callous with their words, and how they mocked them for believing that they were special to Jesus. Their neighbors heartlessly reminded them of how He had healed so many that were sick and oppressed of demons, and here He was not too far away and had not even rushed to see about the family who was so close to His heart. Is this how He treated those that He said He loved so well? She sat remembering how hard she and Martha argued with them and had tried so hard to assure Lazarus that the Master would come in time. Her heart had ached and ached with each passing hour that He had not come.

As for Lazarus, he had grown worse physically as well as emotionally as the delay wore on. She remembered watching her brother's suffering, and this single thing, was what made it so difficult for her to accept the Master's decision to let her brother die. Even now, after all of these years, she still struggled with the idea that the Master would have allowed the one that He loved to burn up with fever, asphyxiate on his own blood, and drown in body fluids. In her estimation, the town's people had been right. When you truly love someone you don't let them suffer like Lazarus had been allowed to suffer.

"Mary," Peter spoke her name so softly to interrupt her thoughts, that she jerked her head towards him, momentarily allowing him to catch sight of the long-held sorrow in her spirit.

"Yes, Sir..." her voice trailed off. "May I ask you an unfair question?" queried Peter.

Mary smiled at him. They had been friends for many years, and she loved Peter with all of her heart. There were many who misunderstood his ways, and resented his gruff manner. She nodded and Peter continued when he saw her smile.

"There were two other people who were raised from the dead by Jesus before He raised your brother back to life. Those two people are seated here tonight," he said as he looked from Hadassah to Josiah.

"You knew about this, correct?" Mary nodded in the affirmative at the Apostle's question.

"And yet, when we arrived at your village, within a stone's throw of your brother's tomb that day, you did not believe that Jesus had the ability to raise Lazarus from the dead."

It was a statement rather than a question, and both women began to see the truth of the matter at the same time.

"In fact," continued the Apostle, "I remember how the two of you met the Master with the charge, 'had you been here, my brother would not have died.' Do you remember saying those words to our Lord?"

Both of the sisters peered at Peter stunned, for he spoke a great truth. Not only did they know of the two miracles from the dead, but they had been hot topics of discussion in their very home! They were beginning to see the Apostle's point, but Martha was still struggling to yield her old contention. Peter continued the line of questioning, for he was determined to see this old wound healed once and for all.

"Martha, do you remember the Lord's words to you when He asked you if you believed that your brother would live again?"

Martha nodded remembering how flustered she felt with the reply of Jesus. He was not one to toy with her emotions, but on that day, His tendency to speak in riddles annoyed her on the occasion of her brother's burial. He had said to her, 'Your brother shall rise again,' rather than saying, 'I will raise your brother.' When she looked back on the happenings of that day, it was the thing that caused her the most angst. She privately felt that if He had simply said that, she would have believed. She was wrong of course, and the Apostle was about to show her to what extent.

"Yes, I shall never forget it as long as I live,"came the flat response from Martha, "and I in response said to Him, 'I know that my brother will live again in the final resurrection of the great day.'

Peter nodded remembering her words as well, and nudged her, "and what did the Master then say to you?"

Martha could respond without hesitation, for the next words of Jesus had been something that rarely left her mind after all of these years. Even now, she continued to turn them over and over again in her heart, as deep things called to the deep.

"He said to me," she continued as she lifted her chin with tears running down her cheeks, "I am the resurrection, and the life: he that believeth in me, though he were dead, yet shall he live, and whosoever liveth and believeth in me shall never die. Believest thou this?"

Then, wishing to justify herself, Martha added, "But I also said to Him that even then I knew that whatever He asked of God, that God would give it to Him."

Peter looked now as Martha was beginning to yield the old issues that cast shadows over her soul.

"Tell me now, Martha, at what point did you first believe?"

Martha could only stare at him as old vines of sour grapes began crushing inside of her under the press of truth. This time, she buried her face in her hands and her sobbing was that of a woman who was tired of carrying the weight of offense. The point was lost on no one who sat there listening. It was obvious that in spite of the fact that she knew that Jesus had raised others from the dead – and in spite of His plain words to her that He was the embodiment of the resurrection and the life, and in spite of the fact that He had shown up, she was offended that He had not come to prevent the death of her brother.

This time the Apostle turned to Mary.

"Mary," he called her name softly again, who had reached to console her sister.

This had been such a long day for both of them, but the Apostle was unmoved. There were still a number of issues that he had to deal with here that night, and he considered himself only half way through his task. Mary nodded her consent to continue the questioning that was now re-directed back to her.

"Tell me something about your brother Lazarus. Was he a believer?" asked the Apostle.

She was almost embarrassed to admit the fact that Lazarus wasn't, for fear that she would speak ill of her dead and beloved brother. She locked eyes with Peter, refusing to concede his point.

"Is it not true," continued Peter in spite of her refusal to answer, "that he never believed that Jesus was the Son of God come down to us in the flesh, even up to the point of his very death?"

Still Mary stared at him without willing to yield, although she had been the one who had anointed the feet of Jesus and washed them with her hair.

"Tell me, Mary," Peter continued, "when did your brother first believe?"

Now both of the sisters had been reduced to tears. Mary trembled as she wept and finally began to see the truth that there had been no other way for Lazarus. He loved Jesus with all of his heart and for so many days of their youth. When they were young boys growing into adolescence and then adulthood, he had never once seen Jesus perform a miracle, never once heard Him claim to be the Son of God, and never once seen Him do anything that explained His sudden and extraordinary change when He reached the age of thirty.

Jesus parted company with Lazarus in their trade of carpentry, and even distanced himself from his own childhood friends and acquaintances in Nazareth. Mary remembered how much this offended Lazarus. Sure, he had been a witness to the miracles of Jesus after His public ministry had begun, but did not for one moment believe that He had affected these cures by some supernatural power or strength. When asked how he believed Jesus did these miracles, Lazarus sincerely could not answer, although he did not believe as the Pharisees did that it came from a devilish source.

Had Jesus not been his familiar as a child, perhaps Lazarus would have been able to make the leap from friend to disciple. As fate would have it, he simply could not believe that the very human Jesus whom he'd grown up with, could also be the Son of God, born of a woman, and be son of his father Joseph as well. Everybody in the room that night came to the powerful revelation that Lazarus had to die so that he could live eternally.

Had he died and not been brought back, he would have died in unbelief. Because he died and was brought back from the dead, he was able to believe and have eternal life as well. It was then that Martha grasped the words of Jesus when He said, 'whosoever liveth and believeth in me shall never die' but this time she finally understood what He was talking about. After Lazarus was raised from the dead, he not only gained new life, but he believed.

If all of this were not enough, Peter was not finished, but he paused and momentarily lowered his head. Truly he loved these two women and understood the weight of all of this as well as the great insult that they had endured earlier in the day at the objectionable demand of the Pharisees. Now he spoke to all of those present because he needed to drive the point home.

"When Jesus declared to all of us that He was planning to go back into Judea, His words were so strange. He told us that He was going to wake Lazarus out of his sleep, and initially we misunderstood His words. We thought that He had changed his mind about going to heal him, until he made it plain to us that He knew Lazarus was now dead. We did not realize that he was not only dead but in the grave for three days!"

Peter paused so that the words could sink in, then he continued.

"Then He said to us," Peter paused for a second to remember the words of Jesus so that he could quote them just the way Jesus had spoken them, *"And I am glad for your sakes that I was not there, to the intent ye may believe; nevertheless let us go unto him."*

"You see, the issue of believing was not just an issue for the household of Lazarus, but for us as well. Though we walked with Him, were taught of Him, we followed Him, and were willing to die with Him, we still did not know who He was. Yes...we saw the miracles, we participated in the feeding of the 5,000, I walked with Him upon the water of the Jordan, and we were there when He opened the eyes of the blind, healed lepers, and made the lame to walk. In spite of all of what we witnessed with our own eyes, we still did not know Him as the resurrection and the life! Those of us who were hand-picked to be His apostles, followed Him without revelation."

Peter groaned from the weight of it all.

The Apostle turned to Martha and Mary again; both had stopped weeping now and there was something in their countenance borne of deliverance that would linger there for many days after this night.

"When we got to the tomb," Peter continued, "and the Master began to weep, many of those who stood by thought that He was weeping for Lazarus. What foolishness! Can you not see the depth of the unbelief from all connected to Him? Why would the Master weep for Lazarus? He had delayed His coming so that He could raise him from the dead!"

Peter spread his hands in a gesture very common for him when he was making an appeal for logic. Eber smiled gently at him, because he had become so attached to the Apostle that he too had taken up the same habit when making a point. Everyone now stared at the Apostle, each struggling to understand this point he was making.

"From the time that the Master was crucified by ungodly men and the time that He rose again and came back to us for forty days, He always had to deal with the issue of our lack of believing! Can you not see that? All of you?" he pleaded with them now.

"Even when He gave us the proof of signs and wonders, we still did not believe!"

The Apostle paused for a moment to re-gather his strength, for this had been a long day for him as well, and like it or not, he was not getting any younger.

Everyone sat eagerly waiting for Peter to continue, hoping that the story would shed some light on why the Pharisees would want to examine the grave clothes of Lazarus on this second time around.

"If you will remember," Peter addressed his statement to the sisters of Lazarus, "when you met us near the city gates, we were close to the catacombs. I remember that even then, none of us really believed that He would raise Lazarus from the dead, although He had said that He would very plainly. We saw Him raise Hadassah and Josiah, no doubt, but His delay in coming to Bethany made us think that Lazarus was appointed unto death although He had plainly said to us that it was not. When He began to weep, we knew that it was not for Lazarus, but it puzzled us, because we truly did not know for what reason He groaned and wept."

Peter grew sad at the next memory, and shared it in halting speech.

"I remember the only other time I ever saw Him weep. His time was at hand and we were headed here toward Bethany and Bethphage. We had come to an area near the Mount of Olives, when the crowds spread their garments on the ground before Him as He rode upon a young colt. They began to worship Him with loud voices and great joy. They cried out to Him, 'Blessed be the King that cometh in the Name of the Lord. Peace in heaven, and glory in the highest,' they shouted it out to Him and made the ground shake with their praises!"

Peter paused for a second when Mary interrupted him.

"This was after my brother was raised from the dead and the Pharisees plotted to kill him, was it not?" she queried.

"Yes, it was," Peter responded.

"In fact, it was soon after that we learned that Judas had already betrayed the Master for the price of a slave."

Peter paused again, this time to remember what he had intended to say before Mary interjected her question.

"The Pharisees rebuked Him," Peter continued, "when the people cried out to worship Him, and I remember that the Master said a strange thing on that occasion. He told the Pharisees that if these were to hold their peace that the very rocks on the ground around them would immediately cry out and worship in their stead."

Peter shook his head in deep thought and admiration. He had witnessed Jesus speak to the wind and water as well as walk on it. There was no doubt in his mind that if the natural elements could be silent at His command, then surely the rocks could speak at His command.

"On that day that He stood at the Mount of Olives and spoke to us, I remember how He said that we, as a people, had missed our day of visitation. When He came to us in the form of a man, He brought peace. In that we rejected Him as our Messiah and our Savior, He warned us that we would always be hounded, mistreated, and have to suffer many things at the hands of our enemies. That is when I saw the Master weep the second time. I saw him weep for the first time at the tomb of our brother, Lazarus."

Peter looked about the room this time and raised his voice so that all would know the importance of what he was about to say.

"Now that you understand that He did not weep for a man that He was about to raise from the dead, tell me all of you, do you think it was because of the Pharisees that He wept?"

Peter's voice held authority as well as indignation. He was driving home a point that was central to the purpose of the gathering there that night. He wanted to be sure not one of them missed it. The small congregation all nodded their heads to indicate their dissenting opinion.

"Then tell me, Clopas, for what purpose did the Master weep?"

Clopas sat staring at Peter dumbfounded. He had been sitting there with the others, quietly taking everything in. When the Apostle turned suddenly and directed the question to him, he knew instinctively that it was not rhetorical. This of course, distressed him to no end. He still couldn't fight the urge to treat Peter as a celebrity, but now he felt put upon and embarrassed, and wished that the Apostle would turn his focus back to the sisters of Lazarus.

When Eleazar saw that the Apostle had suddenly turned his interest to Clopas, it puzzled him deeply. He could see that there was something that Peter was determined to uncover in his friend, but for the life of him he could not figure what that could be. This time Peter turned to Eleazar and looked him directly in his eyes as he answered the question that he had put forth to Clopas.

"He wept because those who knew Him best, witnessed His miracles first hand, and sat at His feet and heard His teachings...did not believe. He wept and groaned deeply in His spirit," continued Peter with great passion, "because He stood at the grave of Lazarus, weighed down by the unbelief of His own disciples. It was the first time I ever saw Him cry."

At this, the aged Apostle bowed his head in sorrow.

CHAPTER EIGHT

The Apostle had been seated too long in one position and had to pause to shift his body weight to a more comfortable position. Most of those who sat around him were not many years younger than he, although he was by far the oldest. His head - full of thick, curly hair - had long since turned a dewy white, and there were deep furrows in his forehead just under his eyes from too much time spent in private reflection.

The hands of the now aged fisherman bore the scars from old cuts and wounds, but the skin was tough and ashen. Although he muttered under his breath, and you couldn't tell whether he was praying or rehashing a sermon, he had none of the mental maladies that marked old age. His mind was as sharp as a trap door. He could share something with you that was quite humorous, but then in mid-sentence drop a powerful revelation that left you staring at him in wonder.

Though deeply sentimental, and oddly emotional at times, none of the high-strung quirks of his personality from the early days were still apparent in the elder statesman. The Lord had known that a much-matured Peter would become a formidable force in the foundation of the Church, and Peter had not let Him down.

Peter continued his story. "When we got to the tomb and He asked which tomb belonged to Lazarus, they said unto Him, 'come and see.' As we moved toward the tomb that belonged to our brother Lazarus, there was a great stone that had already been rolled across the opening of the sepulcher where he had been laid. Those who stood by openly criticized the Master and rebuked Him for healing others but allowing Lazarus to die. The whole atmosphere around the tomb that day was thick with skepticism, unbelief, mockery, and blasphemy. We did not know it at the time, but there were spies in the group as well. They were not there because they cared for Mary and Martha, or because they had come to pay homage to Lazarus. They had come because they suspected that Jesus would come on the scene eventually, and had been sent to report back to the Pharisees anything that He did or said. Can you imagine?"

Peter looked around at the eyes staring at him, and stated, "they had more faith in what our Lord was capable of than we did!"

At this, the Apostle chuckled out loud – but he did so alone.

"As the Lord began to weep because of the unbelief of his own disciples," Peter continued, "He ordered the stone to be taken away. Martha you spoke for everyone standing there when you reminded our Lord that Lazarus had been dead for four days and would stink by then."

Martha and Peter nodded to each other in agreement at the memory, and Martha who had undergone a profound change at this point added a memory of her own.

"He reminded me," Martha interjected, "that if I would only believe, that I would see the glory of God. Peter, you are so right, but I never fully appreciated the depth of the cross He bore until this night. He walked among us as Savior and Life Eternal, but we did not recognize Him as the very Son of God. In that we did not believe that He was sent of the Father, we really never benefited from all that He was. He was Deliverer. He was Peace. He was Restorer. He was Resurrection. He was the Life-giver. He was Savior. When He walked among us, we only knew Him as Healer, Friend and Master."

This time it was Martha who looked around and included the congregation as well as herself in the declarations. Peter nodded his concurrence and took note of the fact that Martha was now a free woman. Every winding chain had been shattered from around her soul, and as he peered at her with keen, discerning eyes, he knew that she would soon meet her own death in this new-found peace. Peter picked up where Martha had left the story.

"He did something that day that taught me a profound truth. He stopped and prayed to the Father. I remember His words so clearly, even to this hour of my life. He lifted His eyes to the heavens and said, 'Father, I thank thee that thou hast heard me. I knew that thou hearest me always: but because of the people which stand by I said it, that they may believe that thou hast sent me.' Then, He lifted His head and with a voice of earth-shattering authority, He cried out for Lazarus to come forth."

At this, both Hadassah and Josiah involuntarily leaned forward at the words of the Apostle. They had such a close affinity to the death experience that the retelling of Lazarus' miracle from the dead resonated with them in a way that was impossible for the others to relate to.

"Where there had once been an atmosphere charged with unbelief and mockery," continued Peter, "there was a power so great that day in the catacombs, that had the Savior not called the name of Lazarus so as to single him out, there would have been a general resurrection of all who lay dead. I remember so clearly when Lazarus came forth," reminisced the Apostle with a twinkle in his eyes. "For a few moments, nothing happened and we all stood there waiting. I remember how powerful the stench was from the open tomb once they rolled away the stone, and everybody there – with the exception of the Master - covered our noses from the smell of rotting flesh."

At this, both Eleazar and Hadassah turned to look at Josiah who was having an epiphany of his own.

"The anointing in the air that day was most unusual, and later on as we all sat at meat, we mentioned this to the Master. I remember how it made me tremble."

All at once the Apostle became very animated as he continued the story of the raising of Lazarus.

"After a few moments… a man that had been dead for four days came hobbling out of the tomb with white linen strips bound about his feet and legs, and a death shroud that covered him from head to feet. Just under the shroud, his head and face were bound with the burial napkin of the dead, and he stood there unable to walk or see. All at once, there was a great tumult as nobody could believe what they were seeing with their own eyes. Some ran in fear, others fainted, still others cried out in wonder and alarm, but those of us who had walked with the Master and called ourselves His disciples, finally believed. He commanded that Lazarus be loosed from his grave clothes."

Mary picked up the story to give Peter a moment to rest.

"Lazarus was a changed man after that. He became a believer and was a believer up until his death on yesterday. From that day forward, my brother followed Jesus with a pure heart and became a disciple and a worshipper, and never ceased to give God glory for the great miracle that occurred in his life. People would come just to look at him to see if he was still alive, and he would welcome their curiosity and would even let them touch him. He seemed unaffected by their demands to know what he had seen and heard while dead. Without cease, he taught in the synagogues of Galilee and Judea, and worked tirelessly to disciple others who were caught in unbelief and doubt as he had been. In fact, he was the one who was so effective with the sisters and brothers of Jesus. You know, they had not even accompanied their mother Mary to the cross of the Master. Our brother Lazarus seemed to see them as his own private assignment, and as he appealed to them as one raised from the dead to eternal life, they received his witness regarding the deity of our Lord and became believers and disciples themselves."

Both Josiah and Hadassah knew of this discipleship of Lazarus and had each wondered in amazement at his willingness to use his notoriety in such an unselfish way. While their lives had been choked and robbed by the weight of their celebrity, Lazarus had used his to point the sick, the lame, and the oppressed to the power of God to change a life. On many occasions, both Hadassah and Josiah had heard that he was in a nearby village or town and would go hear him speak or watch him pray for someone. They each had taken note of the fact that he was not just a man who had been brought back from the dead, but there was a power and anointing on his life that was palatable. There was a blessing just to be in his presence and to hear him tell the wonder of God's grace and mercy. He would even give witness of how he had once walked in doubt and unbelief, but then he would share about how he now was able to see.

"Peter," this time it was Martha who spoke, "can you shed some light on all of the rumors which abound? You said you had something to say to us that would help us understand why the Pharisees made their demand today."

Peter nodded at her and glanced about the room at the others seated there, for he knew that the matter of the grave clothes of Lazarus was at the heart of their great interest in hearing him speak.

"When our Lord was Himself risen from the grave and came back to us for a period to regather us and admonish us, He gave me a command to feed His sheep. At first I thought I knew what He meant, but He knew full well that I did not understand the price. It has cost me everything to obey Him."

The Apostle sighed heavily, thinking of his now deceased wife and his children whom he rarely saw.

"One day, while we walked along, Lazarus followed us from a small distance. The Master spoke to me of my manner of death – He shared with me that I would die an old man, having to be led about like an old stubborn mule."

At this, Peter turned and smiled at Eber.

"All of us had been curious about Lazarus because we wondered what the manner of his final death would be. It was then that the Master rebuked me and asked me why this mattered to me. He stated that if Lazarus tarried until He came back, what was that to me? There were many standing by who heard His words and misunderstood what He said. They immediately began to spread the rumor that our Lord said that Lazarus would never see death again. But that is not what the Master said. What He said was, 'If he tarry til I come, what is that to thee?' This rumor became so wide-spread and common that for a time I also believed that your brother would not die again."

Eleazar was the next to speak.

"Peter, can you offer us some understanding of why the Pharisees would demand to see his grave clothes? If they truly believed the saying that Lazarus would never die – as we all have, now that he is without a doubt dead - why do his grave clothes now matter to them?"

You could have heard the sound of a pin drop from anywhere in the house. Peter turned toward Mary and Martha as he gave an answer that would shock them all.

"It is nothing more than a ruse. It is not the grave clothes of Lazarus that they seek. It is the burial shroud of our Lord that they believe has been in the possession of Lazarus all these years. On the morning that the women went to the tomb of Jesus to anoint His Body for the burial, the stone had been rolled away from the mouth of the tomb and the burial shroud of the Lord was left in the sepulcher, along with the head napkin. The Pharisees got wind of a rumor that Lazarus took the shroud of our Lord and has been buried in it. They have come to demand possession of what they believe is the shroud of Jesus so that they can take it and destroy it forever. They wish to destroy the one remaining article of proof that our Lord rose alive from the dead!"

CHAPTER NINE

There were several people who could have taken the burial shroud of Jesus. It could have been Mary of Magdala, for she was the first one there and also the one who ran to tell the disciples that the Body of Jesus was no longer in the tomb. It could have been Peter as well, because although Lazarus outran him to the tomb, he was the first one to have entered the tomb and actually handled the grave clothes of Jesus. Mary, the mother of Jesus, could have taken it because she was in the group of women who went to the tomb to anoint His Body. Joseph of Arimathaea, the man who owned the tomb in which Jesus had been laid to rest, could have taken it because the Body of Jesus was given to him after the crucifixion. One of the soldiers could have taken it as proof to Pilate that they had not lost the Body as a result of falling asleep. One of several of the women who accompanied Mary to the tomb could have taken it without anyone suspecting otherwise, including Salome, the sister of Mary the mother of Jesus. Lazarus was of course a likely suspect, for he also entered the tomb of the Lord after Peter did, and would have had access to the burial garments. One thing was for sure. Somebody had taken the grave clothes of the risen Lord and kept it a secret.

"Do you think that we buried our brother in the burial shroud of our Lord, Peter? Is that what you wished an audience with us to talk about?"

Mary was not only offended but appalled by the emergence of this new rumor.

"My dear," Peter responded calmly, "I did not ask you here tonight, rather, you are the one who sought me out. I am here tonight specifically to speak to Josiah and Hadassah about an entirely different matter apart from any rumors about your brother. But just so you know, it has always been rumored among the Pharisees that Lazarus was the one who took the burial clothes of the Lord. It initially created a great deal of contention among the eleven of us who walked with the Master and we all wanted to know the truth of what happened to His shroud."

Josiah was intrigued by the revelation that the sisters of Lazarus had not heard the rumors that their brother was the one who had removed the burial shroud of Jesus from the tomb. In and about Bethany, they'd watched Lazarus grow old, and therefore the rumors about him never dying seemed pointless, at least to him. But here was Peter saying that the missing grave clothes of Jesus had become a matter of contention among the disciples, and that Lazarus was the one that they long suspected of having secreted the shroud to a place unknown. Josiah's plot went into overdrive, but not before Peter threw him one more curve.

"Clopas," Peter spoke his name so quietly, that in the midst of the intrigue and swirling speculations, he went almost unheard.

"Clopas," he called him again, and this time the whole room grew quiet.

"When did you first believe?" queried Peter of the man who once begged alms for his livelihood.

"I...I....why, I don't know what you mean. I too honor the works and life of the good Master," Clopas stammered.

A sweat broke out over his brow and he felt that his heart was pounding a hundred miles a minute. As Peter stared at him, Clopas wondered if it could truly be possible that after all of these years and the multitudes of people the Apostle would have encountered, if it were possible that he might remember his shameful secret.

"Eleazar," Peter turned all at once toward his host, "Tell me, when did you first believe?"

Although the question surprised Eleazar, it did not put him off as much as it did Clopas. Without stammering, Eleazar responded, "I first believed when I once made my home in the catacombs with nine other lepers. One day Jesus healed all ten of us, and tonight I gained my freedom from guilt and shame. Although the Master healed all ten of us, as you well recall, only one returned to give Him thanks. I wish I could say that one was me. Nonetheless, I have freely admitted my failure before my children and these new friends of mine," nodded Eleazar toward Josiah and Hadassah.

"When the Lord cleaned me of my leprosy, I believed; but tonight I have become a disciple." With that, Eleazar choked back fresh tears.

"As for Clopas, he can answer for himself," continued Eleazar, "but I tell you a truth, I have known him to be a good man, by all accounts, and I can attest to his hospitality. He uses the great wealth that he has acquired at the temple gates to give alms to those who are less fortunate than himself."

As Eleazar sang his praises, Clopas was looking for a way to make a quick and respectful exit from the presence of the Apostle. Peter nailed him to his seat with piercing eyes.

"Tell me, Clopas, when you first met Jesus, was it at the same gate that you begged alms of me and John?"

As the aged Apostle watched him closely to see if he would yield, Clopas bowed his head low upon his chest, and began to weep silently. The room was stiff with disbelief. When would Clopas have met Jesus, and why had he never mentioned it? Although it was a question on everyone's mind, it was Eleazar who now carried the greater offense.

Clopas began his story in halting speech and amidst tears.

"There is a disease that has run in my family line for many years that affects the bones and muscles in the legs and feet. I was not the only one of my family that has been healed miraculously. My brother was also healed by the Master in the city of Nain. When he was healed, he insisted that I be moved to the temple in Jerusalem so that I too could be healed. When they began to lay me at the Beautiful Gate of the temple to beg alms, the offerings of silver and gold increased to the point that I became a very wealthy man. You must understand, Peter, that up until that point, I was no better off than a leper. I had been chained to my disease all of my life. I never felt much like a man. I was as a helpless child who is unable to do for himself, and must be carried about and cared for constantly. Sometimes I had to lay in my own filth until someone was kind enough to come and take me home."

Clopas looked around the room, seeking some small degree of sympathy.

"The day I first saw Jesus at the Gate Beautiful, was not the first time that I had met Him. I had seen Him many times. I had been a part of the thousands and thousands who had thronged Jesus looking for a miracle. But…"

Clopas paused before saying what he was about to speak, knowing that once spoken, there was no way to take the words back.

"But, I began to get so much money from the alms at the Beautiful Gate, that I…I…I was reluctant to be healed by the Master for fear that I would lose the means of my living. I knew that if the Master healed me, I would no longer be able to beg. You must try to put yourself in my place and understand how bad my life had been."

This time Clopas looked all about him and half pleaded, "How was I supposed to take care of myself? I had no trade, no other way to earn my way in life. Begging had been my whole life. I did not know anything else to do."

Josiah grew exasperated by the need of Peter to interrogate everyone in the room about their past sins. *Who gave him the right? And who cared anyway? What could any of this have to do with what happened to the burial shroud of Jesus? That is what he wanted to hear about!*

"Soon after I was moved to the Gate Beautiful of the Temple," Clopas continued, "the Master noticed me among the crowd of sick and infirmed who had gathered there to beg alms as I did. One day He picked me out of the crowd…it was the strangest thing!"

Clopas hesitated as he recalled the memory.

"I never reached out to Him or cried out to get His attention because I struggled with the fear that if I got healed, I wouldn't know what to do with the rest of my life. I have no idea why I was singled out by Him. But He did. One day He walked right up to me – past many others who were also lame – some even blind. He asked me if I wanted to be made whole. I couldn't believe He spoke to me apart from all of the others who wanted to be healed so badly…"

This time the voice of Clopas trailed off as he sat lost in thought between self-condemnation and sadness.

"Clopas!" Peter spoke his name as if in rebuke, but mostly to get his attention.

"Do you understand what the Master meant when He asked you if you wanted to be made whole?" queried Peter.

"He wanted to know if I wanted to be healed, of course," replied Clopas.

"If it is true that to be healed is to be made whole, then tell me my friend, were you made whole on the day that I touched you?"

Peter peered at him waiting for the deliverance to come. All at once, Clopas broke down and began weeping again, but not from pity.

"No…no…I don't believe I have ever been whole at any time of my life," stammered Clopas in remorse.

"You all sit here talking of grave clothes and burial shrouds…I feel like I have been bound in grave clothes all of my life. My legs were made whole on the day that you grabbed me and lifted me up," he said peering from Peter to the others, "but I still wear a burial shroud of my own. I have worn it since the day that I refused the Master's offering of something greater than silver and gold."

Although Clopas dropped his head at this, there was something going on in his heart that was bringing him to a place of repentance and restoration.

"Clopas, when our Lord raised Lazarus from the dead, even he was given a choice about what he would do with his new life. He could have merchandised it much as Josiah has done, and even Jairus, the father of Hadassah, or he could do what we now celebrate most about his life. What you received through me and John on the day you were healed was good. What the Savior offered you was better. Had you accepted His gift, you would have received healing and eternal life as well. You would have been made whole. One day you will see the Master again, and hopefully you will have more to show Him for the life you have lived than what you have to show right now. Your trinkets and baubles will profit you nothing when you stand before Him at the judgment seat in the resurrection," Peter spoke the stern words with great emotion and eloquence.

"Peter, tell me please, what must I do to receive eternal life? I have lived with this self-loathing all of my days, and I want to be free this very night. Please, tell me what I must do to cleanse my heart and to be made whole?" cried Clopas.

Hadassah was so greatly moved by the words of Clopas because she had long experienced the weight of feeling beyond redemption. Tonight she was free, and as she sat watching him, she began to pray that God would do a second miracle in the life of Clopas.

"You have even now spoken it my friend," said Peter with a slow smile.

"You see, Clopas, Jesus did not heal every lame man that He encountered, nor did He heal every leper," stated Peter glancing at Eleazar.

"He did not raise every dead widow's son," he stated looking at Josiah, "nor did He bring every dead little girl back to life at a father's request. There were many sick and diseased people that our Lord stepped over."

Peter stopped momentarily to let his words sink in. And sink in they did with Clopas. His tears were not the tears of remorse or regret anymore, but they were tears of release and cleansing. As the change began to work itself from his spirit to his soul, he realized all at once, that although Peter healed him of the disease in his legs, he had remained crippled in his thinking. He had not walked out a life of deliverance after his miracle. He had remained sitting where he always sat on his pallet at the Gate Beautiful begging alms. Tonight, he was free in his mindset, and not just healed of his disease.

Now Peter looked at him and allowed him the space for true worship from his heart.

"Clopas," Peter said to him softly, "tell me one thing more. Who healed you at the Gate Beautiful on the day that John and I met you?"

Clopas looked at him and got the message very quickly.

"Jesus did. He gave me a second chance. Thank God for second chances," he whispered.

"My brother," said Peter, "then give Him the glory! Your healing did not come from the touch of a man – it came from the touch of the Master."

"I remember a day when our Lord touched the eyes of a blind man. When the man's eyes were opened, the Master asked him what he could see. He told the Master that he saw men walking as trees. I remember it so well," chuckled Peter, "well…when he said that, the Master gave the blind man a second touch. Sometimes, Clopas, our first encounter with Christ is not sufficient because we are not ready to fully surrender the profit that is attached to our crippled limbs. Still, in His mercy and grace, He extends His favor to us in so many ways –

along with His forgiveness! Every now and then, after the Lord heals us, we still need a second touch from the Master in order to be made whole."

"Peter, we must go now," it was Martha who spoke with finality in her tone. "My sister and I are very weary, and tomorrow is a new round of mourners and guests. May I speak freely concerning our desire to see you tonight?"

Peter spread his hands before them in his signature gesture, "I don't see why not, say on, my dear."

This time Martha sighed as she spoke.

"You must forgive my earlier contention. I meant you no harm, for you shall always be welcome in my home as a brother, and not just a friend."

Peter nodded at Martha's words.

"We are concerned that the Pharisees will come during the night or by other means of subterfuge and desecrate the burial place of our brother Lazarus. They not only demanded that the tomb be re-opened, but they demanded to inspect his burial shroud. Of course, they would never defile themselves in such a way, but they have sent their henchmen to do their wicked deed. Even if such an absurd thing could have occurred as Lazarus being buried in the shroud of Jesus, how would they know our Lord's burial shroud from any other? One burial shroud looks just like another."

Martha looked tired as well as overwhelmed.

"Not exactly," stated Peter in a flat voice.

"I myself saw and handled the burial shroud of our Lord. When Joseph of Arimathaea received the Body of our Lord from the Roman soldiers at Pilate's command, he packed the Body of our Lord with spices and wrapped it in the burial shroud immediately after he received it from the cross. Because it was the high Sabbath, no one touched the Body of our Lord to cleanse it until the morning that the women went there to prepare it for the burial. When Mary of Magdala came to us and told us that the stone had been rolled away and that our Lord's Body was no longer there, Lazarus and I ran to His tomb immediately. I went in first and examined the shroud and head napkin before anyone else did, including your brother. There were multiple stains of the Savior's blood on the areas which covered his feet and ankles, as well as a large stain of blood where the soldier drove his sword through His side. There were also stains of blood where the blood from His pierced scalp had dripped down and pooled around his face, neck and shoulders."

Peter was forced to stop a moment to take a deep breath. Although the crucifixion of Jesus had occurred many years before, and he understood that His death on the cross was to bring redemption to mankind, remembering the details of his beatings in the Judgment Hall and the cowardice of the twelve had never been easy.

"The blood was never washed from His burial shroud," Peter continued in a quiet voice.

"That is why they want to examine your brother's burial garments. They know that the shroud which belonged to Jesus will still have his blood stains from the crucifixion."

Eleazar and his daughters stared at Peter in amazement, Clopas looked on bewildered, Mary and Martha appeared numb, Hadassah couldn't believe what she was hearing, but Josiah was in calm, deep thought. In his estimation, clearly Peter knew exactly where that shroud was.

"Just for the record," Martha stated as she stood and addressed all who were assembled there that night, "my brother was not buried in the shroud of our Lord. If anybody should know, my sister and I definitely should know what he was buried in! We never even knew that such a shroud existed until this very night. If my brother knew of such a burial garment and its whereabouts, he took that secret with him to his grave."

With that, Mary and Martha rose silently, wrapped themselves in their outer tunics against the chill of the night, and did the best they could to conceal their faces as they returned to their home. Several spies observed them as they left the house of Eleazar the merchant.

CHAPTER TEN

Clopas left the home of Eleazar soon after the sisters of Lazarus did. And so did Peter, to the further astonishment of Josiah and Hadassah. He seemed to have changed his mind about talking to them concerning the business that brought him out that night, and even Eleazar sensed that Peter had more to say to him as well. As Eber ushered the older man out, Peter turned one last time to all of them and peered from one to the other.

"On tomorrow, I shall speak more about the purpose of my visit here tonight. For now," he sighed, "we all need to take our rest. We have a very long day before us, and the enemies of our Lord are already underfoot with their devices."

As Josiah and Hadassah were each directed to their sleeping quarters in the home of Eleazar, neither was able to get much sleep that night. Hadassah was a changed woman for sure, but the talk about grave clothes and secrets bothered her, placing a damper on her new-found peace of mind. Josiah, on the other hand, was neither bothered nor changed. The information he was able to garner from Peter clarified a few matters that had nagged him about the rumors of Lazarus, and deepened his conviction to move forward with his scheme.

Both awakened a few hours later to the smell of the morning meal. It was a simple and traditional breakfast of curds, hot bread and goat's milk, but was sufficient to fill the heartiest of appetites. Hadassah joined the women of the house as they busied themselves in their morning chores of spinning, weaving, and mending, and Eleazar was already up and about preparing his cart of wares. Josiah found him folding fresh new rolls of textile of wool and flax that had been prepared by his daughters in beautiful colors and patterns. He pushed and shoved bottles and jars of assorted perfumes and fragrances into a pleasing arrangement that would be easy to sell. Though his mind was on his deliverance from the night before, he worked quickly and mechanically to prepare for the day's receipts.

Hearing Josiah's approach, he turned to greet him and was surprised to see that he was dressed to make a departure.

"Is Hadassah safe in your home, my friend?" Eleazar met his eyes and nodded in the affirmative.

"Josiah, whatever you are planning, please consider what this woman has been through all of her life. God has wrought a mighty deliverance of liberty in her life…I would hate to see her hurt…"

Josiah raised his hand to cut Eleazar off, "I have no plans to hurt her. I would hurt myself first before I would do anything to compromise her virtue or cause her harm. You have discerned correctly that I have an interest that involves her help, but it will fall out to both of our advantages and not just my own."

With that, Josiah turned to leave and Eleazar turned back to his work. *Whatever Josiah was planning*, he thought to himself, *would benefit no one but himself – that was for sure!*

"Father, are you coming in to eat?" asked Tamar, interrupting his thoughts.

Eleazar turned to glance at his beautiful young daughter. Every day she looked more and more like her mother and some days he found himself staring at her amidst feelings of grief and loss. He knew that it was time for him to pay the dowry for betrothal, but Eleazar was loath to lose her. It was their custom for the elder daughter to marry first, but Dinah had refused to consider marriage again after the young man she had become betrothed to died suddenly of a mysterious illness. She felt cursed and had gone about in mourning garments for many years afterward. Eleazar had hoped that the Apostle Peter would have ministered to her as well on the last evening. In his opinion, she needed to be free of grave clothes as well.

"Of course, my dear! It appears that one of our guests has taken an early departure," stated Eleazar.

Tamar groaned her disapproval. Although she had just met Josiah and Hadassah the night before, she felt connected to them in some strange way. They both felt like family to her and the opportunity to cook for them and fuss over them had brought warmth and goodness to their household. As Eleazar entered the main entry of his home, he stopped for a moment, startled by the sight of Hadassah. His staring embarrassed her, and she quickly drew her shawl around her head to cover her face.

"Hadassah," Eleazar stated her name gently and affectionately, "you have no more need to hide your face. You are among friends, and what God has done for you on this past evening must not be undone by the modesties of womanhood!"

At that, all of the women laughed heartily, including Hadassah, but she left the veil pulled about her face just the same.

"Eleazar, I am going to the home of Mary and Martha this morning. I was deeply troubled by the news last night that the Pharisees would violate our laws by desecrating the tomb of their brother over a burial shroud!"

Hadassah said it in genuine displeasure.

"Of course, my dear," replied Eleazar, "but be careful on the roads today. When I went out last night to speak to Eber, the servant of Peter, I saw what I believe were sentries from the Sanhedrin. What they lack in principle and honor, they more than make up for in their craftiness," replied Eleazar.

"I can smell them a mile away. They must have followed Peter here, and realized their good fortune in having the sisters of Lazarus show up here as well. I am sure that they believe that something with respect to the shroud is afoot. Be very careful how you carry the rumors that you heard here last night," Eleazar warned her as he clutched her hand.

"Did Josiah say where he was headed? He told me last night that he would be here in Bethany for a few days for the mourning period of Lazarus," Hadassah queried, as she deliberately chose to ignore the topic of discussion from the night before.

She had some suspicions of her own about the burial shroud, but had never discussed them with anyone. She wanted to discuss what she'd heard about the shroud from her father Jairus, but now she was reluctant to speak to anyone except maybe the Apostle.

"He did not, my dear, but he was very concerned about your welfare, and wanted my assurance that you had a place to lodge during your stay here in Bethany. You are of course welcome to stay here for as long as you like. You are a part of us, and should always feel welcome to come directly to my home when you have business here in the village," replied Eleazar.

As Eleazar spoke, Hadassah opened the hand which clutched her veil, and allowed it to fall from her face.

"Thank you so very much Eleazar. You are a blessed man, you and your wonderful daughters. May God show you the same kindness as you have shown his handmaiden," replied Hadassah.

"And we pray God's grace and peace to you as well," they all responded in unison.

"Hadassah, please make it a point to come back and see us again and tell us how you fare!" added Tamar.

The women hugged and fussed over her as they led her to the door, reluctant to allow her to take her leave. When Hadassah left the household of Eleazar on that day, she was never to return, but the memory connection of her soul-cleansing with the household of this dear man and his daughters would last for the balance of her days.

She was lost in thought as she made her way through the crowded streets of the hamlet of Bethany. It was a warm, sunny day and she paused often to peer into faces and was astounded to see that no one recognized her as the daughter of Jairus who had been raised from the dead. She noted to herself that when one is free of grave clothes, the spirit of death leaves as well. She was dressed in mourning and planned to join the processional of mourners who would once again make their way to the tomb of Lazarus with his family members at the head of the gathering. She couldn't make up her mind, however, if she wanted to go first to the home of Mary and Martha to join the processional there, or go directly to the tomb. It was while she jostled the wisdom of either course back and forth in her mind, that the elderly woman who had stepped in front of her and recognized her at the tomb of Lazarus, once again crossed her path.

"Hadassah."

The woman spoke her name as a statement rather than a question, and acted as if Hadassah was a compatriot to something. When Hadassah looked up, with her face completely uncovered, she was surprised to see the familiar face of the woman who had frightened her terribly on the day before. Hadassah looked all around her, remembering the earlier warning of Eleazar, and nodded to the woman acknowledging her identity.

"How do you know me, and do you mean me any harm?" queried Hadassah in the bluntness of her father Jairus.

"I mean you no harm, Hadassah. I am Sarah of Bethany, and was healed of the Master on the same day that He raised you from the dead as a young girl."

This time it was Hadassah's turn to block the path of Sarah.

"Please, walk with me to the market place. I have something for you to see," the old woman spoke it with an insistence, and Hadassah was so eager to meet someone who was connected to the story that Peter had shared last night about her resurrection from the dead, that she willingly fell in step.

Hadassah deliberately slowed her pace for Sarah who was much older than she and who also walked with a funny shuffle, but appearances are most always deceiving. They were quiet as they walked, but Hadassah kept turning to steal glances at the woman who was known around the region as the one who had lived a life of humiliation and uncleanness. Her twelve year issue of blood had confounded the doctors in Judea as well as Galilee, and made her the central theme of local gossip and hearsay. As a very young girl, she had often heard her mother speak in whispers to the other women in the village about Sarah. Amongst themselves, they had decided that Sarah was being punished by Yahweh for some terrible sin that her parents had committed.

"You are not hiding your face today, and there is something drastic that has happened to you," Sarah said it with a twinkle in her eye.

"Tell me, Sarah, how did you recognize me?" queried Hadassah. "I am no longer a young girl of twelve, and you appear to be the only one in Bethany who even knows that I am still alive."

Sarah nodded at her as she also nodded to many others along the way. Those that met them on the tiny cobbled streets of Bethany never spoke her name, but they would wave at her and even reach out to touch her as if she were someone highly favored among them.

"I can never forget you. Do you want to hear my story?" queried Sarah.

Hadassah nodded eagerly and noticed that people would peer in her face as if they sought recognition. They seemed to envy the position she occupied in the old woman's company.

"I didn't die the death that you, Lazarus, and Josiah did, but I lived twelve years in a tomb nonetheless. I passed the years of betrothal and child-bearing in great mourning and grief, and felt that God had not only cursed me but was bent on punishing me for a wrong that I could never remember that I had done. When I was a young child, about the age that you were when you were brought back from the dead, a near-relative violated me and took my virginity. Something strange happened to me as a result of that beating and violation. I came down with a number of emotional and physical ailments, and even developed tumors and growths on my female organs. I suffered greatly at the hands of physicians who tried to uncover the source of the inner growths, but gradually the growths turned into bloody flux and I was the walking dead even while I lived."

The old woman paused as she relived the anguish while Hadassah remained silent to listen and learn.

Sarah continued. "No one knows what I suffered, and even now it is very difficult to speak of those days that were filled with so much pain. You know, I was a young woman then, and had the dreams of a young woman. I was my father's only daughter. After my disgrace, my father Hezron was disgraced as well. They talked of stoning me to the elders of the village, but my father was held in great respect among them and he was very wealthy. For his sake, they would not hear of it and refused to believe the tales that I had brought this crime upon myself as a result of loose morals. Can you image? I was but a girl of fourteen when it happened. My near relative was never punished for the crime that he committed against me. He is still alive, and I am able to go and minister to him with food and staples, and with a heart free of injury or bitterness."

At this, both women stopped to look at each other. Hadassah looked at Sarah in disbelief, but Sarah looked at Hadassah with the discernment that this exchange between them would settle some final issues in Hadassah's soul.

"It cannot be easy," Hadassah remarked with compassion.

"No," replied Sarah, "but it is when the love of the Master so fills your heart, that nothing else can find room."

"How can you possibly speak of love when this man took everything from you? He ruined your life. I remember that as a young girl, we were told not to have anything to do with you or your family. I was told that you were unclean and cursed and that to even speak to you could bring a curse upon ourselves," Hadassah was reluctant to tell it, but she was searching to gain a blessing from this woman's experience.

"I mean you no harm…" Hadassah started to add, but then Sarah stopped her with a smile.

"No, you do me no harm with the memory…it is in my past. It cannot hurt me," Sarah stated with a genuine smile.

"The man that you say took everything from me took what the Master was able to restore! Today, I walk in forgiveness and charity, and I have no regrets that I never married nor bore children." Sarah said it sincerely, but Hadassah was still not convinced.

Secretly, she carried the shame of herself being violated, but the trip to the burial of Lazarus was less about him and more for her wholeness.

"Forgiveness was not about releasing my near-relative, Hadassah, it was about gaining release for myself. In fact, the idea of releasing him would never have been possible as long as he was a member of my father's clan. Every time I looked at him, I could recall the smell of his body and the roughness of his hands. I remember how his violence destroyed more than just my innocence. He introduced me to an adult knowledge of intimacy that created dark shadows in my thinking and my emotions. I never knew what forgiveness could mean to me until I actually forgave this man. It was then that I realized that I had become a prisoner to my own pain."

Sarah paused to think through the analogy that she would now use to help Hadassah understand.

"Think of an onion," she smiled at Hadassah, and the two women nodded that they both had clear, solid knowledge of onions.

"It is made of many skins. You peel back one, then another, and then another. At first, it seems as if you will never get to its center. But if you look closely, each time you peel a layer, you are getting closer and closer to its core. In fact the core is made up of layers – there is no core without the layers."

Sarah looked to Hadassah to make sure that the woman was with her in the image. Hadassah nodded as she was well familiar with onions.

"This violence against me added many layers of female emotion and pain that I was too young and undeveloped as a girl to deal with. Had you dealt only with my rape, you would have missed my sense of rejection by men. Had you dealt only with my rejection by men, you would have missed my self-loathing for bringing my parents so much pain and disappointment. Had you dealt only with my self-loathing, you would have missed my sense of dirtiness and uncleanness. Had you dealt only with my sense of always being unclean, you would have missed the terrible weakness I endured as the blood, which issued forth from my body, always left me wasted and gaunt. I could go on and on about my layers. When you peeled back one, there was yet another and that one was equally dark and horrible. It was better for all concerned, that I had never been born."

At this, Hadassah looked away, avoiding the eyes of her companion. It was difficult to think that anyone else besides herself had ever longed for such a thing.

"The man who took my virginity lied to my father, Hezron, and told him that I had led him on. He mixed just enough truth with lies that although this man attacked two other young girls in the village, to this day my father is unsure of what to believe. I grew into womanhood ashamed and cursed. I was not only a prisoner in my village, but a prisoner in my father's house as well. When the tumors caused bleeding that would not abate, I was not allowed to touch anything in our home for fear that it would render my father and brothers continually unclean. This meant that I couldn't do the simplest tasks without worrying about how it would affect someone else's ability to enjoy life."

The older woman had to pause to catch her breath.

"What made you seek out the Master for your healing? He could not touch you without rendering Himself unclean." Hadassah did not mean it to sound as disapproving as it came out.

"The Apostle Peter later shared with me that the Son of God could never have been rendered unclean. He touched lepers, prostitutes, tax collectors, even Samaritans. None of them had the power to make Him unclean. Rather, He made us clean and gave us life everlasting."

Hadassah nodded and was thankful for the understanding she was getting. She knew that Jesus was the Son of God, but until last night, and this talk with Sarah, she had never fully understood all that it meant to have been touched by the Master's hand.

"My father died and my brothers forsook me. My mother had long since abandoned me emotionally, if not physically. Had it not been for my father's great wealth, I don't know what would have happened to me. It would not have been good. My father's wealth allowed me to seek out a number of physicians. They took every penny that my father left to me, and left me nothing better. I was at the point of complete desperation when I heard that Jesus was passing by. I had lived with torment and a sense of being dirty for so long, but Hadassah, I tell you a truth, there has always been some strange desire to fight locked up inside of me. I remember wanting to fight my relative's lies. In a bold moment, I once demanded that my father bring him before the elders of the city to question him. I remember how my father stared at me unwilling to see his personality reflected in his own daughter."

"I remember scrubbing and scrubbing myself in the mikveh, trying to scrape the dirtiness off. Thank God for it! It was because of that inner fight that I decided to take a chance on the Savior. But it was not the first time I had heard of Him or seen Him. I tried to get to Him once before, but there were thousands of people who thronged Him, and to get to Him would have meant touching others."

Hadassah looked at Sarah and noticed the tears on her cheek, but she did not want her to stop. There was something that Sarah needed to impart to her, that she knew would help her turn a final corner.

"Thank God for your father, Jairus!" Sarah exclaimed.

Hadassah looked at her surprised, for she said it as if she knew her father personally.

"On the day that Jairus came running to the Master, he was crying, exhausted, and desperate for you. I remember that he pushed others out of the way to get to Jesus, and I never saw a man so willing to do anything to get something for someone else."

As Sarah spoke it, Hadassah stared at her. This was a second testimony to the love of her father. He had never shown any affection toward her after she was raised from the dead, and Hadassah had never believed that her father loved her.

"I saw Him when He first appeared. There were so many who were unclean and filthy with their sores and diseases that I was never even noticed in the crowd. This was the second time that I tried to get close enough to Him to touch Him and could not for the press of the crowd. There were so many there pushing and shoving, while others screamed and cried out from their misery. The disciples of the Master would form a boundary around Him so that it was next to impossible to even see where He was at any given moment what with the multitudes that thronged Him. All of a sudden this man fought his way through the crowds and I watched him closely, for I saw that he would give me the opening I needed to get to Jesus. I watched him as he fell at the feet of our Lord and began to plead and beg for Him to come to heal his little daughter who was at the point of death. That of course, was you."

The two women smiled at each other and nodded, but Sarah had to stop once again to catch her breath as they got nearer to the noise and activity of the public market place.

"Our Lord seemed to know your father, and stopped what He was doing to give heed to what Jairus was saying. When He turned and began to follow your father back to your house, He stepped over many, many sick people as He directed His focus on getting to you. This was my moment! As He walked with Jairus, it helped me to maneuver my way through the crowd, which began thinning out. Many of them felt defeated, and stayed where they were rather than fighting to follow Him to the house of Jairus. But for me, it meant I could creep up on Him from behind and just touch the hem of His garment. I did not want to render Him unclean, and I believed – falsely – that He would never agree to touch a dirty woman like me. I got in as close as I possibly could to Him and wedged myself in among a small group of people who still pushed and shoved to get His attention. I dropped down to the ground next to several other people who were close to His feet, and I reached out and grabbed the hem of his mantle."

At this, all of a sudden Sarah stopped in her tracks, but instead of meeting Hadassah's gaze, she stood there remembering, but staring into space.

"Something akin to a lightning strike went through my body all at once. I felt the issue of blood from my body staunch immediately! As the crowd continued to surge forward, I crawled backwards out of His line of vision, and rose quickly to run fast as I could. I tell you, Hadassah, something not only happened in my body, but something surged through my heart as well. It was as if a life-force started from my temple and coursed all the way through to my feet. I didn't know it, but the healing virtue of the Master was stripping away all of the layers of that onion that I had tried so unsuccessfully to scrub away with aloes and water. I was beside myself!" exclaimed Sarah as she got caught up in the memory of her deliverance.

"I tried to run so as not to draw attention to myself – because the virtue from the Master made me tremble violently. But then, to my horror, He came to a complete stop, turned, and began to look in my direction demanding to know who had touched Him. At this point, His disciples began to scold Him – I could not hear what they were saying because of the noise of the people, but I imagined that they were confounded that He would ask such a question with so many sick folks pulling on Him and begging Him for help."

"That is when I took note of Jairus again. He seemed upset that something had deterred the Master. But the Master would not leave it alone. I covered my face and tried to cover my presence with the press of the crowds, but our Lord started walking directly toward me as if He knew exactly where I was. As He walked towards me, I could hear Him say, 'Who touched me? I perceive that virtue has gone out of me. Who touched me?' There were so many that had touched Him that the sick began to cry out the more. That is when I saw someone from your father's household run up to him through the crowd and begin to yell something to him that caused him to rip his clothing and cry in great anguish and distress. The Master stopped to have the household servant repeat the words that he spoke to Jairus, but He also saw me. I tell you, Hadassah, His eyes…the eyes of the Savior saw me that day with the greatest kindness and compassion! I had never known that kind of mercy and compassion as I did in that one moment when He looked at me."

The two women started walking again, but this time grew quiet as they made their way through the midst of the noisy market square. Hadassah did not know where they were headed, but the general direction was a place reserved for those who begged alms. Sarah stopped to pick up a basket for her shopping, and lazily went from one market stall to another, purchasing small items as she went.

When they got to the periphery of the market place and headed toward a sea of beggars who sat before them with their hands spread - supplicating for alms, Sarah stopped once more to catch her breath before continuing her story.

"He stopped a moment to say something to your father, then, all at once, turned His attention back to me. That is when your father looked at me as well. In fact everyone did. I felt naked but unashamed that day. No one knows…no one knows, but perhaps Him. He knew and understood my lifelong shame, for He reached out His hand to me and said, 'Daughter be of good comfort, your faith has made you whole. Go in peace.' I remember that your father stared at me in recognition but also in horror, for he must have recognized me in that moment as the daughter of Hezron. I was afraid that he would disclose my identity and humiliate me for being out in public. But he did not. He only looked at me knowingly, and seemed relieved that the Master was still focused on following him. At this point, we learned you were dead, and one of the twelve said to your father, "Why trouble ye the Master further? The damsel is dead.""

Sarah and Hadassah had come to an area just adjacent to the market plaza where people gathered to beg alms. The place usually reeked of unwashed bodies, discarded and spoiled food stuffs, and open festering sores. Small dogs were also about, licking dirty hands as they too begged for food and picked through the litter. There were so many of them that initially Hadassah balked at the idea of walking among them. But then she realized she had no choice but to follow

Sarah in and among them, if she wanted the gift of this woman's incredible testimony.

"They cannot help the condition they are in Hadassah. They did not ask for this. Who does?"

Sarah said it as a rebuke as she bent to the supplicating hands to give them small packets of food and jars of ointment. The women tried to hide their dirty faces with scarves and tunics that were badly soiled. Their body odors were always the worse.

"After a while you stop smelling them and only see their needs," stated Sarah, this time without rebuke or scorn.

She stood momentarily to give Hadassah some of the items she picked up for distribution, and Hadassah hesitantly reached to accept them. This time as they walked along without speaking, they reached to this one and then to another to give out the items.

As they did, the voices raised in unity to them, "thank you! God bless you! May God show you the same kindness as you have shown me! Thank you! Sarah, God bless you for your kindness to me!"

On and on the chorus of gratitude went, and it began to work itself into a place in Hadassah's soul that had long been closed off. Sarah must have discerned it for she stopped momentarily to bring attention to it.

"When I stopped you at the tomb of Lazarus on yesterday, it was not to embarrass you my sister. That is not my way. I recognized you of course, but I am not one who has respect of persons. It was not your identity that gave me wonder. It was something in your heart that spoke to me of a woman who is intimately familiar with what it means to be counted as useless and worthless."

When Sarah spoke it, Hadassah peered at her and nodded that it was so.

"How did you come to do this? What brought you to these people and their needs which never end?" Hadassah asked.

"My healing and deliverance brought me here," was Sarah's reply.

"After the Lord called me out on the day that you died, and I received that marvelous gift of healing, I wanted to follow Him for the rest of my days. My healing was instant! It did not take hours or days as it did for many that He touched. But the most marvelous thing of all was that when I touched the hem of His garment, it healed me every whit. I was made whole that very moment. The flow of His virtue washed me, cleansed me, transformed me, and brought me new life. You are looking at a woman who was resurrected from the dead."

"From that moment on, I counted every tear drop, every hurt, every moment of shame, every rejection as dung. My life began on the day that He told me what my faith could do. I have reflected and thought on that one particular thing each day of my life. And I have strived with everything within me, to use that same measure of faith to reach out to those who have also been thrust aside to touch them with the Master's compassion."

This time the two women stood face to face as they spoke. They had distributed all of the personal items and food that Sarah had purchased as they made their way through the marketplace.

"Hadassah, a great change has come over your life. I can see it plainly. You are not the same woman that you were yesterday. You are not the same woman that I have seen many, many times over the years. You are no longer hiding your face. And you are no longer in mourning for a life that you long wished for but could never have. We are given what we are given. I once heard the Apostle Paul teach that in whatever state he has found himself in, that he has learned to be content – whether good or bad, joyful or mean, he has learned to therewith be content. I have never forgotten his words. When I find myself sad about something, or looking back with regret, I remind myself that the state I am in can be made better with gratefulness and contentment. Before long, I find that no matter what the issue was that settled heavy on my heart to make me sad, it is gone and replaced with God's peace that surpasses all understanding. It is then that I realize how truly blessed and favored I am."

"It is not the things that we possess that bring us true peace Hadassah," continued Sarah.

"It is the content of our heart – that alone defines our well-being and our sense of self-worth. The heart speaks – rather loudly, and if you have not taught it to be thankful and courteous, it will bully you into living your days in continual unhappiness and misery."

Sarah paused out of respect for Hadassah's flow of tears. The daughter of Jairus had just turned an important corner and was being transformed before her very eyes.

"These," Sarah pointed to the sea of faces and outreached hands which were still extended to them in supplication and begging, "are in every town, village, and hamlet. You need not look far to find them. They are outside our city gates, they make their homes in the catacombs, they make small communities of themselves near every public marketplace, synagogue and even outside the Temple gates. Hadassah, seek them out. Touch them. See to their needs. Wash their wounds. Give of whatever substance that you have to feed them and clothe them. If you do this, you will be our Lord's hands extended. If you do this, you will have thanks enough when you stand before our Lord in the Resurrection. He once said that when you give them a portion of bread or fish, or you give them water for their parched throats, you do it as though it had been done for Him."

Sarah's speech not only touched a nerve with Hadassah, but it gave her an epiphany. It was true that there was something about people who were sad and in distress that moved her emotionally. She had never responded to the unction that such needs triggered in her spirit, however, because to do so would have meant disclosing her identity. But now, strangely, it seemed not to matter as much. As she faced Sarah in a heart now made pure by conviction and repentance, she nodded her willingness to spend the rest of her life providing this ministry service.

"Do unto them as unto the Lord, Hadassah, and I promise you the weight of their desperate needs and even their squalor will never overwhelm you."

Sarah said it with a gentle nod, for she realized that the woman who stood before her would go on to do a work that would never be acknowledged by men as being worthwhile, but would nonetheless gain her a place of prominence in the Kingdom of the Lord.

They began to walk again, and this time Sarah finished her story. She realized that the assignment that the Holy Spirit had sent her to the tomb of Lazarus to accomplish was now done. She had not gone to the tomb of Lazarus on the day before to honor the man or to show kindness to his sisters. Lazarus had often given alms to her for the work that she did with the poor and the infirmed, but she never participated in burial processionals – not even as a measure of honor to the dead. She recognized the prodding of the Holy Spirit when He spoke to her to go to the tomb, and was as surprised as Hadassah when she looked up into the face of Hadassah as she watched her struggle to cloak her identity.

"On the day that you died, which was the day that I gained new life, we became the Lord's daughters! Which means…we are sisters!" smiled Sarah to Hadassah.

Hadassah wiped her tears away and chuckled with Sarah at the saying, for it was entirely true. There was a connection in their spirit that Hadassah felt during the entire time that they walked and talked. She felt as if she'd known Sarah all of her life. What a wonderful and life-changing trip this had been to Bethany. It only proved that when the Lord is in control, even a trip to the tomb can be a divine appointment.

"Where are you headed my dear?" queried Sarah.

Hadassah had to honestly pause to think, for she had not made a decision about which place she should go to first when Sarah stepped out and interrupted her course.

"I think I must go to see the sisters of Lazarus," stated Hadassah.

"There is some information that I have that I believe they need to consider in order to make a decision about the bones of their brother. In a year from now his remains must be placed in the city's ossuary and there is something important that they should consider."

There was a strength and conviction in Hadassah's manner that had not been there before, and this too caused Sarah to look at her and marvel. Sarah chuckled at the strength of character that she saw in Hadassah.

"You will do much good my sister, for you are a no-nonsense woman and a woman who will know how to take little and stretch it to get a lot done."

Hadassah nodded at the saying, for it too was very accurate about her personality. She had even been criticized by her father for being a little too prudent in her business dealings for the household. But she hated waste and knew a thief when she saw one.

"I will walk with you, for we have been followed for some time now." As Sarah said it, Hadassah looked around in alarm.

"Do not be alarmed, they have not followed you to harm you or intercept you, they only want to know who you talk to and where you lodge while you are here in Bethany."

Sarah said it without emotion and this seemed to give Hadassah the calm she needed to proceed with her plan. The warning of Eleazar to take caution in what she repeated of Apostle Peter's words the night before still rang in her spirit. Something in her wanted to bring up the rumors concerning Lazarus that were abuzz in the city, but somehow she sensed that none of it would surprise Sarah. She decided to err on the side of caution and hold her peace about what she knew from her father Jairus as well as what Peter had shared of what he knew.

"After my healing, I followed your father and the Master along with His disciples from afar off," Sarah had picked up the story she initially began.

"I was not simply curious, but I longed to follow the Savior. My heart belonged to Him that day and from that day forth I made it a point to join with the other women who followed Him to minister to His needs. Serving Him has been the joy of my life. And when they crucified Him on a tree, I continued to serve Him by serving others who sit abandoned at the gates of our cities."

"The disciples of Jesus were a peculiar group...today, I understand them better, and I even like them." Sarah smiled at Hadassah when she said it as she remembered the roughness, particularly of Peter, James and John.

She noted that before their conversion, they seemed to dislike the presence of women around the Master, and in her estimation demonstrated a specific dislike for small children. She chuckled to herself as she thought of it. Thank God that as they matured as apostles, they had changed. For the Kingdom of God was made up of small children.

"Peter, James, and John took note of the fact that I followed them, and it seemed to annoy them to no end. But the Master did not mind at all, and at one point turned to rebuke them for their reproach of me. When we got to the house of Jairus, we were first met with the awful sound of the mourners. Someone ran in to tell your mother that your father had returned. I remember that when your mother Azaiah came out, she was the picture of grief and sorrow. By then, you were a young girl of twelve, pronounced dead by your physician. The wailing and the screaming of the mourners created an atmosphere that made you want to give up hope, no matter what you believed about the Master. I remember thinking that all hope was lost – and this was just moments after He had healed me of an issue of blood that had lasted twelve long years. Hopelessness is a powerful thing, Hadassah, I learned much that day about faith when it must confront the power of fear."

What Sarah had just said was a compelling truth, and Hadassah paused as they walked to let the revelation sink into her spirit. She wanted to grasp it and never forget it. This Sarah was a woman of great insight and wisdom, Hadassah noted to herself. What she didn't know was that Sarah had secured both through the crucible of suffering. It had cost her something.

"I have to tell you that even today," Sarah continued, "I have a strong dislike for mourners, burial grounds, and the like."

Sarah said it with a tone of apology, but Hadassah completely understood. It had been the awful sound of the mourners that formed her first memory from the dead when she was pushed back through the chasm too quickly.

"When Jairus saw that your mother had given up all hope, the words that Jesus had spoken to him, 'fear not, believe only,' seemed to lose their power. Can you imagine, my sister Hadassah? The Son of God was there in our presence, and we knew Him not. That, my sister, is what the power of fear can do. You can have the One who can be whatever you need Him to be in that moment of the crisis you are in, standing right there in your defense, and you can still remain in your condition when you fail to see Him as the very Son of God. I remember that when He first went to the tomb of Lazarus at his first death, Martha remarked to Him that she knew that her brother Lazarus would live again in the great resurrection of the dead. The Master corrected her and told her that He was the Resurrection and the Life. That it was not an event, but a Person – and He was that Person. She still did not get it, though." Sarah chuckled at the memory.

"But I was dead… even though Jesus had come," interjected Hadassah.

"How can you resist fear? It is natural to give up hope when circumstances are the opposite of what you have believed for. Surely, when my father went to find Jesus, my mother's faith would have been strong. How can you fault my mother for giving up once the evidence went against what she believed for?" queried Hadassah, for she had a genuine desire to grow from the wisdom of this woman.

"You are wrong if you think that I fault her. I have learned not to judge, Hadassah, for it is a luxury of fools who have not lived long enough. No, I merely state to you a truth that I learned from the teachings of the men of God. You see, fear is something that must be confronted. You cannot give it audience though it yearns to give instruction; you cannot let it walk with you even when it is your daily companion; you cannot let it advise you, even when you know it has given you good counsel; you cannot let it guide you, although it begs to lead you; and you cannot consort with it, even when it promises to be true to you and be your only lover."

The words of Sarah rang true to Hadassah, and she quieted her unction to disagree so that she could gain more.

"What then is faith, and how does it differ from fear?" asked Hadassah.

Sarah paused for a moment and looked her in the face when she answered.

"Fear gains its strength," Sarah replied, "when it is able to train our eyes on what is before us. It anchors itself with the words of your detractors, and if it can get you to yield, it will seek to gain your worship. Faith will look at the same set of facts and the weight of the crushing evidence that fear uses to puff itself up, and faith will stubbornly believe in the impossible anyhow. Faith is something that is strengthened by reason of exercise, experience, and hope. You can't conjure it up out of despair and despondency, and think that it will somehow win your trust. When you are standing in faith about something, you must treat any wavering thought or unction to worry as a sworn enemy. You must oust that thought immediately before it takes root and then gains fertile ground in your mind."

As Sarah said it, she recalled a teaching of Peter. He was teaching a great crowd on one of the hill sides of Bethany years before, when he shared with them his experience of walking on the waters of the Jordan. It was the same day that they had gotten the sad news that John the Baptist had been beheaded. When the news was brought to the Master, Peter recalled how much it affected Him. He had gotten into a ship and departed to be alone in a desert place, wanting to spend some time in prayer. The twelve sought Him out later during the fourth watch of that night, and it was then that they saw the apparition walking on the sea that they took to be a ghost. Peter shared with them how the wind was boisterous upon the waters, and the sight of the spirit walking toward them stirred up every one of their superstitions.

Sarah remembered how Peter said that they all cried out in great fear, and that it was then that they heard the Master's voice say to them, 'Be of good cheer. I AM! Be not afraid.' He told of how he challenged the Master with the words, 'If You are really the I AM, bid me to come to You on the water.' Jesus then answered him with a loud voice and the single word, 'Come!' Sarah remembered how they all leaned forward as little children when Peter spoke, for there was something about his voice and the way that he gave texture and clothing to his words that kept you spellbound, no matter what truth he was teaching. It was then that he imparted the great truth about fear that Sarah had never forgotten. That truth had served her through some of the toughest days of our life, including the deaths of every member of her immediate family.

She remembered how Peter shared that when he stepped out of the ship to walk on the water to go to Jesus, that he said that he did not feel water under his feet! She smiled at the memory of how the entire congregation had laughed at him with delight, and how even the children clapped their hands in joy as Peter had paused in his storytelling to give animation and sound to the memory of standing on water. But then, she recalled, he said that all of a sudden the wind became very unruly as he made his way to Jesus, walking on the sea.

He explained to them, and Sarah paused as she walked with Hadassah to reflect on it, that it was when he took his eyes off Jesus and gave his worship to the wind, that he started sinking. He said that he cried out for Jesus to save him, and that at this point the Savior was close enough to him on the water that he was able to stretch out His hand to grab Peter. He told of how the Master said to him, 'O thou of little faith, what caused you to doubt?' Sarah remembered how effective that story had been when Peter taught it. He explained to all that heard him that day that to fear something, is to give it your reverence.

Hadassah could see that Sarah was lost in thought, but they had now made it through the center of town and were so close to the house of Mary and Martha that the sound of the mourners were now in hearing distance.

Sarah stopped now and faced Hadassah and then suddenly changed the subject. She knew that these last words of counsel to her would serve her well in the days ahead. Hadassah felt it too, and was saddened that their discourse had come to an end. She was now not only a changed woman, but a woman set free of an assortment of private demons that had kept her bound and chained for more than forty years.

"Hadassah, when you forgive, it does not mean that you are saying that the person who committed harm to you is not guilty of their crimes. In fact, when people harm you, they incur a debt that they can never repay. Why? Because they can never go back in time and undo what they should never have done or said in the first place. And it doesn't matter who they are or what their relationship to you may be. Sometimes the crime is made more difficult to bear because of who they are."

Sarah paused long enough so that Hadassah could allow the parade of faces of those who had caused injury to her to walk across her memory.

"There is no question that they have injured you in a way that can never be restored," Sarah continued. "But when you forgive, what you are saying is that you drop the charges against that person who could never repay the debt they have incurred against you, no matter how hard they tried. Sometimes we temper our decision to forgive on whether the person says they are sorry. But of what consequence is that? Does it change the great harm that they have done through their ugly words and the crime that they have committed against your person? How does 'I'm sorry?' repay their debt? If you would be honest with yourself, 'I'm sorry' does not repay. Rather it will drive you to further wrath, because you can't help but want to demand – with their apology – the reason for the injury they have committed against you. Do you not see that it only deepens the wound?...it does not bring you closure to have that person admit to their wrong."

Hadassah stood there with conflicting emotions. She knew that Sarah spoke the truth and that it was time to let go of her need to know the answer to the many Whys of her life.

"Forgiveness, my sister, is actually a very selfish matter. For the one that you ultimately free is yourself when you forgive an injury from the heart. I used to think that forgiving meant that I was somehow condoning the wrong. What I have learned is that forgiveness means taking away that individual's power to ever hurt me again. I am the one set free through forgiveness – whether the one who harmed me gets free or not. When you will not forgive a crime, that crime is repeated over and over in your heart as well as your mind. That is why to recall it is to relive it. To be free of the pain, you must free yourself of the thorn, and the only way to do this is to forgive. This is what the Master taught us. He taught us that we must forgive others who hurt us if we want Yahweh to forgive us, or else we are doomed to always walk as victims. Can you understand what I am saying, Hadassah?"

There was a plea in Sarah's question, but there was an anointing to it that one could feel.

"My dear sister and companion in the faith of our Lord Jesus, I bid you Godspeed in the grace and mercy of our Lord. I charge you this day to be instant in season and out of season. To minister with your whole heart and with the substance that has been entrusted to you, to those who are in need much as the Savior has commanded us to do. With everything that is in you, be at peace with all men. Redeem the time, for you have much living to make up for. In the City of Jerusalem by the sheep market, there is a pool called Bethesda. It has five porches. Do you know of it?" Sarah asked Hadassah. She nodded to the older woman that she did.

"In these porches," continued Sarah, "lay a great multitude of sick, impotent, and diseased people who wait for the annual troubling of the water."

Hadassah knew the place well and required no further description. She, as well as most people, took great pains to avoid going anywhere near the place.

"There is much there that your hands will find to do."

Sarah said it with finality to her voice, but then just before she turned to walk away, she added as a final afterthought, "And Hadassah...whom the Son has set free, is free indeed!"

As Hadassah bowed in deep respect and genuine love for the wise older woman who now turned on her heels to walk away, she wept fresh tears of gratitude and thanksgiving. Hadassah stood for many moments watching Sarah walk away with her peculiar shuffle, but as she did so, a covert movement in her peripheral vision forced her to refocus her thoughts. She gathered her wits and headed for the house of Mary and Martha, as she took note of the fact that there were three strangers in Bethany who could be seen standing in the distance watching her every move.

CHAPTER ELEVEN

A knock at the door sent Eber scurrying, but Peter looked up from his work completely indifferent to the interruption. He was expecting several guests that day, and had made it a point to ready himself for the private agendas that each would bring to his table. Although he hated subterfuge, he knew how high the stakes would grow once his revelations about the burial shroud of Jesus became part of the rumor-mill of Bethany.

"I have been expecting you. Please come in," Peter looked up to greet Josiah as he stepped into the small alcove where the Apostle was seated with several scrolls of parchment scattered around his feet.

He had come a long ways from the unlearned fisherman who could neither read nor speak well when Jesus chose him to be one of the twelve and prophesied to him that one day he would be a fisher of men. Since that day, he had not only become a pillar of the new-found movement who called themselves Christians, but had become one of its most respected rabbis.

The disorder around the feet of the Apostle gave the whole room a look of untidiness, and momentarily Josiah paused to look around to choose an unencumbered place to sit. As he sat on a nearby stool at the beckoning of Eber, he had to work hard to hide his annoyance. It bothered him to no end that the Apostle seemed to know his every thought even when he was quiet.

"Do I annoy you, Josiah?" the Apostle asked it with a touch of sarcasm.

Eber nudged the Apostle with a gentle rebuke as he swept up extra parchments and incomplete letters addressed to several churches that they had been writing before Josiah knocked on the door of Reuel, the Potter. Both Peter and Josiah were well advanced in their years, but neither was feeble- minded, and each could be blunt to a fault.

"Peter, I believe you know why I have come. I am a man who has no use for the games that children love to play," stated Josiah in a flat, even tone.

The words came out a little harsher than Josiah meant them to, but he need not have worried about causing offense to Peter. He was already way ahead of Josiah, and was about to throw him one final curve that would cut the visit short and give way for a small group of Pharisees who would be his next visitors of the day.

"It is interesting that you would use the description of a child playing games," replied Peter. "You have come into Bethany with something hidden in your hands behind your back, and you have gone from this one to that one to see if anyone can guess what it is you have in your hands. Is that not a child's game, Josiah?"

The Apostle peered at him now a bit testier, but he was not going to allow Josiah to disrupt his calm. Josiah sighed heavily, willing to concede the line of reasoning.

"You have something that I am willing to pay a handsome price for," started Josiah.

"You mean the burial shroud of our Lord?" queried Peter to cut to the chase.

Josiah nodded in the affirmative.

"I do not have it," came the flat response from Peter, "and if I did, I can assure you that it would not be up for sale. Tell me something, Josiah. What plans have you made for Hadassah?"

Josiah sat for a long moment staring eye to eye with Peter. *This one*, he thought to himself, *was not to be toyed with. He could see through walls.*

"If I tell you the whole truth for why I have come here and how it involves Hadassah, will you agree to give me any additional information you have about the shroud and not hold anything back?" pleaded Josiah.

It was a long shot, but Josiah came to the realization that if he hoped to gain anything from Peter, it would have to be on the Apostle's terms.

"No." The response was flat, emotionless, and clearly non-negotiable.

"I am planning to warn Hadassah about you myself," began the Apostle.

"In fact, she is headed here later on today. And when she comes, I plan to expose your scheme to her. I would advise you to get to her before she comes to me, because if she hears it from me, your plot will not go well."

"Rabbi," Josiah used the term with genuine respect toward Peter, "I have not come to hurt Hadassah. She is of age. She is more than free to deny the request that I will make of her. What harm do you believe my plan will cause to anyone?"

Josiah sat there waiting for an answer from Peter, and when it was clear that no answer would come, Josiah decided to go for broke.

"I knew nothing about the burial shroud of the Master until the day that Lazarus died. When the news of his death came to me, I prepared to make my sojourn here to pay homage to his family out of a pure heart. Although I have known of his life and his service to our Lord, I have never exchanged a single word with him. All three of us who were raised from the dead by the Master have been united in life by this rather odd happenstance. We have been involved in each other's lives from a distance, and I suppose through some unspoken pact as well. It would be difficult for anyone of us to explain it, and even Lazarus has journeyed to look after my welfare as well as that of Hadassah's. It is the only reason that I thought of Hadassah in my ultimate plan to acquire the shroud."

Josiah paused in his story to gauge the interest of the Apostle. Although Peter sat expressionless, he was listening very closely.

"During my preparation for the journey here to Bethany, I received a visit from a small group of scribes and Pharisees. To say that their visit alarmed me would understate the fact. I wanted them to state their business quickly and leave as I did not want anyone to see them in my home and start a rumor that I was in anyway a friend of theirs."

Josiah stated it hoping to win an appeasement from Peter, but it didn't work. Peter was unmoved. Josiah continued in his effort to show all of his hand to the Apostle.

"They shared with me that they had long since believed that the Body of the Lord had been stolen out of the grave by the disciples of Jesus. A Roman soldier, who had been sent to the empty tomb of the Master to inspect it, took back a report to the Pharisees that Mary of

Magdala was both the first and the last person to have entered the tomb of Jesus. It was their suspicion that when she met with all of you after the resurrection of the Lord, that she had His burial shroud in her possession."

Josiah paused to once again measure the reaction of Peter. There was none, but there was interest, for some of this Peter was hearing for the first time himself.

"If they truly believed that we stole the Body of our Lord from the tomb, then of what consequence does the burial shroud have for them?" queried Peter.

"They were greatly disturbed when the Body of the Lord could not be found," answered Josiah, "for they accused all of you as His disciples of using the missing Body as a ruse. They felt that you would try to use His burial shroud to make the case that He left it behind when He was raised from the dead. They were also concerned that the same power that He used to heal the sick and raise the dead, would somehow be deposited in the burial shroud. They want to take possession of the shroud so that they can destroy it, in order to put a stop to the Lord's Movement forever."

Peter couldn't help but shake his head at all of the nonsense.

"They expose the real intent of their evil devices," Peter said with exasperation. "If we were going to use His abandoned grave clothes to make the case that He had risen from the dead, why would we hide it? Would we not have made His burial shroud an object of worship?"

Peter spread his hands wide in an appeal for logic from Josiah.

Josiah had not thought of that one himself, and nodded to Peter that he agreed. "Say on," responded Peter to Josiah.

"Well...," continued Josiah, "of course, I wanted to know for what purpose they had come to me. You remember Nicodemus and that he was a ruler of the Jews, as well as a follower of Jesus, of course?" Peter nodded attesting to the accuracy of the facts.

"They shared with me that before Nicodemus died, he shared information with his good friend Jairus, about the whereabouts of that shroud. Evidently, Mary of Magdala had been approached and threatened about the shroud, and she confessed to Nicodemus – whom she considered a friend and a disciple - what she had done with the shroud for safe keeping. Whatever Nicodemus learned from her, they do not believe he took with him to the grave. They wanted me to use my influence with Hadassah to find out what her father Jairus learned from Nicodemus. They offered me a handsome price for either the shroud or information that would help them obtain it, but I am not interested in providing them with either. I want the burial shroud for myself."

With that, it was Josiah's turn to wait on Peter.

"How does Lazarus figure into this intrigue?" asked Peter.

"They don't know for sure," responded Josiah, "but they suspect that it was given either to Lazarus or to one of the Lord's disciples. They knew how much the Lord loved Lazarus, and have always leaned toward believing that Lazarus is the one who took possession of it and has had it all of these years. They believe that on his request, his sisters buried him in it."

Josiah at least now benefited from an open dialog with the Apostle, and was glad for that, even if he could gain nothing more.

"You are a man of God, Rabbi, you know whether I am speaking the truth," offered Josiah, this time spreading his own hands before Peter.

"So far…so far. Say on," responded Peter.

Josiah continued. "I personally believe that the burial shroud of our Lord has healing properties in it. If our Lord was raised from the dead in it, then the shroud can effect miracles."

Peter chuckled as Josiah said it.

"Do you think," started the Apostle, "that it was His burial shroud that got Jesus up from the dead after three days?" asked Peter.

Josiah, who had been initially offended by Peter's laughter, now stared at him as the logic became very apparent. Peter, on his part, knew that the stakes had grown too high to continue to allow Josiah to nurse his preposterous scheme.

"If the power of the shroud is what got Jesus up from the grave, why did it take three days?"

Peter asked it leaning forward to drive home his point.

"It was not the shroud that raised Jesus from the dead, Josiah! And I tell you of a truth, there is no healing power whatever in the burial shroud of our Lord. I touched it and handled it for myself."

This time Josiah was quiet, and Peter saw that the news deflated something in the heart of the man who sat before him.

"What was it then that raised Him from the dead?" asked Josiah, as he peered into the face of Peter wanting to know the truth.

"The answer to that, my friend, will set you free," is all that Peter would respond.

With that, Josiah stood from where he was seated, and left the presence of Peter with a heavy heart. He did not get what he had come for, and now wished that he had not come at all. The logic of what the Apostle had said about the shroud made sense, and Josiah could see that if the shroud had any power at all to raise the dead, clearly Lazarus had not been buried in it after all.

CHAPTER TWELVE

Although Hadassah was now a greatly changed woman, she wondered if she would ever get delivered to the point that she could tolerate the wailing sound that mourners made. They stood outside the home of the sisters of Lazarus, and kept up their vigil of noise – and this, without let up. The group was made up of women shrouded in black, and as they screeched and flailed their arms, the loose fabric of their garments gave them the appearance of buzzards about to take flight. Sometimes they would stoop to pick up dirt, and they would stand with streams of it pouring from their hands, while they threw clouds of it towards the heavens. As a child, Hadassah had never quite comprehended the need for such an eccentric drama troupe at a funeral. It just seemed to her that there was always enough grief to go around without them. She remembered how they had gathered so quickly at the home of her parents, before she had even died.

At her approach, several turned to search her face for recognition, but that did not seem to affect their clamor. They were able to wail and scrutinize visitors all at the same time, and Hadassah took note of the fact that there was not a real tear anywhere in the bunch. Martha was the first to greet her, and it was a hearty one at that. The two of them grabbed each other as sisters would have, and met each other's eyes with a gentle nod. Martha had been eyewitness to most of Hadassah's transformation, and was sincerely grateful that she had come.

"Thank you for coming, my sister, and is it well with you today?" asked Martha.

Martha guided Hadassah into her home while she spoke, and motioned for her sister Mary to join them.

"It is well with me, and I pray with you as well. How does this day find your household Martha?" Hadassah responded.

Hadassah studied the face of Martha as she said it, and took note of the deep circles under her eyes which was an indication that she had probably not gotten a good night's sleep. Mary also swept Hadassah up in her arms, and they all looked around for a private place where they could talk.

"Let us go up to the roof for a moment," stated Martha, "Hadassah, is there something that we can get for you to eat?"

Martha had been freed of many obsessions as she had matured into an old woman, but hospitality was not one of them. The two sisters steered Hadassah through the small group of friends who had gathered there for the traditional period of mourning, and were greatly relieved by the distraction that Hadassah's visit had brought. When they got to the roof of the spacious home, they found mourners there as well. Mary signaled to them that privacy was needed, and the assembly disbursed immediately to return to the main house.

"Mary has always been good at getting rid of people," Martha said it with a twinkle in her eye.

All of the women chuckled at this, and it gave Hadassah the signal that she needed that she did not have to be sad. A great work had been wrought in her soul as well as her life, and she refused to spend another day of her life being sad about anything.

"I came to Bethany to pay my respect to your brother Lazarus, but my coming here today was for an additional purpose," began Hadassah.

The two sisters nodded as she spoke, for they had something to share with her as well.

"I am fully aware that Josiah has private intentions of his own, although I am still not clear how he plans to involve me. The Apostle gave me needed insight to the many rumors that are afloat in Bethany about the interest in your brother's grave clothes, although I do not believe that it is his grave clothes that you should concern yourself with the most."

Mary and Martha both nodded at once, for they also understood that there was something more concerning the rumors of their brother that they were still not aware of. Most of it did not make sense to them that the Pharisees would commit such a sacrilege to their customs and traditions as to handle the grave clothes of a person committed to the grave.

"Please continue, Hadassah, we want to hear all of it," replied Martha.

"My father Jairus was a close friend of Nicodemus," began Hadassah.

"Although Nicodemus was a Pharisee, he was also a disciple of the Lord and a believer. Not many would know it, but it was Jairus who encouraged him to seek out Jesus. He had heard the Master speak on many occasions, and his heart was open to change. The two of them – my father and Nicodemus – were like brothers until the day Nicodemus died. My father is a very old man now, and from time to time he forgets that his friend is dead, and will ask for him to come. I have to remind him that Nicodemus is dead, and this never fails to make him sad."

Hadassah paused to gather her thoughts.

"When the Master was crucified, there were as many rumors in Judea and Galilee about the whereabouts of His Body as there are right now about the grave clothes of Lazarus. My father and Nicodemus were as distraught about the crucifixion of our Lord as any of those who loved Him. There was great fear as well as distrust in Jerusalem after the Master was taken and bound, and the disciples were not the only ones who forsook Him in His hour of need. To admit that you were an associate of the Master even in private conversation was risky, and the Pharisees were looking to take your brother to kill him as well."

As Hadassah reminded them of the danger that Lazarus had been in, both sisters remembered how they had begged Lazarus to restrict his public movements. It had no effect on him and he stubbornly refused to live in fear of what the Pharisees might do to him.

"Yes," interjected Mary, "when they took the Master and bound Him in the Garden of Gethsemane, my brother followed the soldiers to the judgment hall of Pilate. Although all of the other disciples forsook Him, save Peter, my brother was no longer afraid of death or dying. He was a changed man when he came out of the grave, and was willing to follow Jesus even if it meant going back to the grave."

All of the women paused to consider Mary's words, for Lazarus' life had been wholly devoted to the teachings of the Christ once he was brought back from the dead.

"When he and Peter got there that night," Mary continued, "the servants of Caiaphas the High Priest recognized Lazarus immediately because of his great fame as the man who had been brought back from the dead. Peter was able to gain entry that night into the Judgment Hall as well because of Lazarus who insisted that the servants of Caiaphas allow him to come in."

It was a detail that Hadassah had not heard reported, although she did remember that her father, Jairus, had shared with her that all of the Pharisees had been eager to call Lazarus to interrogate him after he had been raised from the dead. They had not only followed his every movement with spies, but were as fascinated about looking at him and asking him about his death experience as everyone had been in Bethany. Hadassah continued when she saw that Mary had concluded her remarks.

"Apparently, when our Lord was risen from the grave, it was the Body of our Lord that first caused the distress of the Pharisees. They did not have full knowledge then that Nicodemus was a disciple. When they met to discuss the talk that Jesus had been seen alive after His crucifixion, they talked freely of their fears before him. The whole purpose of crucifying the Master was to kill His purpose and wipe out His Name. They had even sealed the mouth of His tomb with a stone that took a band of soldiers to move – and that with pulleys and chains. Can you imagine how they must have felt when the soldiers that they left there to guard the tomb could not say what happened to His Body? Can you imagine how they felt when our Lord was seen alive in the Holy City, walking and talking with His disciples for more than forty days?"

The women looked at each other greatly encouraged by the talk, and Hadassah felt that she had finally come to truly love the Lord in just these few hours that she was released of her chains.

"They must have been astounded when they received the reports that He was seen not only alive and in the flesh, but that He still bore the scars where the nails had been driven through His hands," added Martha.

"Yes," continued Hadassah, "I remember that my father reported that at first, the Pharisees tried to make light of the reports and said that the people must have seen a ghost. But when Nicodemus saw the Master himself, and even sat with Him at meat, he refused to try to hide his allegiance any longer. He was no longer interested in hiding his conversion and openly declared that he was a disciple of the Master. Of course, they could not have one of their own declaring that he was in league with the One that they had dared hang on a tree, and so they threatened Nicodemus to silence. From that day forth, he refused to walk with them, and became a constant visitor to our household. After his death, my father once sat with me, and shared some information that I think the two of you should know," said Hadassah.

"Say on, for we are anxious to hear it," Martha spoke in a low tone for she was well aware of the fact that all of them were being followed by spies.

She had her suspicions that even some of those who were lounging about in her home that very moment in the guise of mourners, had probably been paid well for any reports or information that they were willing to provide the Pharisees. She noted early on that the mourners seemed overly occupied in studying the face of every visitor to their home. Her sister, Mary, was the one who sat at the feet of Jesus to learn His truths. She, however, was the one who ran the household and kept provisions in the house, and didn't have to be bitten by a rat to recognize one supping at her table at meat.

There had been a throng of people at the tomb of Lazarus on the day of the processional to the tomb. She and Mary had been astounded by the size of the crowds as well as to learn the great distances that people had traveled to get there. As the one who was very street-wise, she assured Mary that it was not because they loved Lazarus and had come to pay him homage. Rather, it was because they wanted to see if there was any truth to the rumor that he would never die. She had been glad to see a few of the apostles of Jesus there, including Peter, and had half wished that they would do an all-out call for repentance. Peter laughed at her when she suggested it, and opined that it would take over a week to cast out so many devils.

Hadassah continued with her story.

"I was greatly intrigued by the report of Peter last night that he could recognize the burial shroud of our Lord when he sees it, for it had never occurred to me that it would still contain the blood stains of our Lord."

Both Mary and Martha nodded their heads up and down in unison, for they too had been fascinated by this detail.

"My father Jairus shared with me that it was Mary of Magdala who removed the shroud of our Lord from the tomb and delivered it to Peter when she was threatened by the Pharisees," explained Hadassah.

The mouths of both of the women fell open at this news, for he would be the logical choice. Mary of Magdala had died some years before, but had continued to follow the apostles to assist them and serve them long after the death and resurrection of the Lord. She had been very close to the inner circle of Jesus, which was made up of Peter, James, and John.

"Mind you," Hadassah continued, "I don't know if in fact that is true, for I have never shared this information with anyone before now and have no way to test whether it is true. But there is more."

This time Hadassah paused to wait for the encouragement of the two sisters, for she knew that all of this must have been a lot to handle. She reached out and touched the hands of both of the sisters and squeezed, for she regretted that she was there to share rumors at such an occasion as the death of their brother. Both of the sisters, then reached to comfort Hadassah, for the issue of their brother's death did not cause them the sorrow that most people thought. Martha was the one who verbalized it for Hadassah.

"Please, we need to know what you have to share with us. Do not be swayed by the tumult of the mourners, our brother Lazarus lived a full and wonderful life. We do not weep for him as those who have no hope, for we shall see him again. We had the opportunity to see him deal with his private demons about the deity of the Christ and from the day that he came out of the grave, he never ceased to preach Jesus and the power of His shed blood on the cross to anyone who would listen. He and the Master had once been the closest of friends...even as brothers...but after Lazarus was brought back from the grave, he embraced Him as the very Son of God."

Hadassah nodded and was glad for the reassurance. She reached up momentarily to touch her face, as a single tear ran down her cheek. She realized that she too had come to know the One who brought her back from the dead as the very Son of God. Just for a quiet moment, all three of the women looked up to the heavens in worship. They realized then that there was an unseen Host who also sat with them, who had come at the very mention of His Name.

"Nicodemus claimed," Hadassah continued, "that the Pharisees made a pact that they must do whatever was necessary to retrieve the bones of Jesus. They believe that Peter presently has possession of the burial shroud, but they are convinced that Lazarus had His bones. With His bones, they would then prove forever that the Master was an ordinary man and that the reports about Him rising from the dead in a body of flesh rather than a ghost to be false."

Just saying it, left Hadassah breathless, and all of the women stared at each other in disbelief.

"What in the world would my brother do with the bones of our Lord, and how could anyone ever identify whether they were truly His?" asked Mary.

"My father did not want me to make this journey to Bethany because of what I am about to tell you. He told me that it was rumored among the Pharisees that when you gather the bones of your brother to place them in the ossuary a year from now, that you will by stealth, also place the bones of Jesus there as well so that He will finally have a proper burial."

Hadassah finished the reporting with a sigh.

"What nonsense!" stated Martha as she struck the palm of her hand in vexation.

"How does it help them to demand to examine my brother's grave clothes?" queried Mary in a small voice.

"I believe it is a ruse," stated Hadassah.

"I believe they want the bones of Lazarus to prove that the rumors that he would never die again are false, and that they also desire the bones of Jesus so that they can prove once and for all that He was an ordinary man. But it is only my opinion. My father is a very old man now, and his memory goes in and out. Sometimes he does not even know who I am. I try to keep him as comfortable as possible, but his death is imminent, I know. I don't know what worth any of this information from him is to you, but this I do know....he and Nicodemus would sometimes whisper well into the night, and I often felt afraid for both of them," concluded Hadassah.

"Is there anything more, Hadassah? You must tell us everything you know," said Martha.

"Josiah has some part in all of this," shared Hadassah, "although I am not sure why he thinks that I would cooperate in any way. I am sure that he knows how close my father and Nicodemus were years ago, and I am equally sure that he is probably in conspiracy with the Pharisees about something. He said to me on last night that he never knew about the existence of the burial shroud of our Lord until he received news of your brother's death. He did not say who gave him that news," concluded Hadassah.

The three women sat for a long time in silence, just reflecting, thinking, contemplating, and finally shaking their heads at the rumors that were now rich fodder for the gossip mills of Bethany. The two sisters realized that there was nothing that they could do to prevent the desecration of their brother's tomb. The two of them had decided privately that they must not tax themselves over the theft of his burial shroud or even his bones. They knew that the tomb would never hold Lazarus, for they had once heard the Apostle Paul say that *'to be absent from the body, was to be present with the Lord.'* The Lord had taught them that when a believer died, they received a new body. He told them on several occasions that it was needful for the mortal body to take on immortality. Lazarus would be raised from the dead with a glorified body that would not contain bones or sinews. The old earthly tabernacle of their brother was no longer able to contain his spirit – he was truly free now – he would never die again. What's more, he was now reunited with his boyhood friend in Paradise.

As Hadassah shifted her weight so as to come to a standing position, Martha reached out and pulled her gently to indicate that there was something more to tell.

"There is something that we feel that you should know as well. Do you have more time?" Martha asked. Hadassah nodded.

"Josiah beat you here this morning," stated Mary in a small voice.

"He left just moments before you came," added Martha.

"He tried to act as if the information that the Apostle Peter shared last night was the reason for his visit, but we knew that it was only a ruse. When he finally left off of the formalities, he was very forward in terms of what he was really looking for," Martha looked at Mary as she said it.

"He caused us quite a bit of offense when he demanded to know if we had in fact buried Lazarus in the burial shroud of our Lord," stated Mary.

As Hadassah took it in, she felt a mixture of anger as well as disgust.

"He did what?" demanded Hadassah.

"Yes," continued Martha, "he finally revealed his intentions for being here in Bethany, when he demanded to know if the rumor about Lazarus was true. He told us that he had heard that the burial shroud has healing properties and that he believed it was the shroud that raised Jesus from the dead."

Martha said it in a flat, expressionless tone this time, but one could see how tired she was.

"What did you tell him?" queried Hadassah.

"The truth of course," answered Mary.

"We told him that we did not bury Lazarus in the burial shroud of the Lord, and that the first we had heard of such a shroud was from the Apostle last night."

Hadassah looked from one to the other of the sisters and asked, "What does he want with the shroud?"

Martha peered into her eyes and said, "He wants to purchase it for his own use. He confessed to us that the Pharisees had first approached him when he made ready to come here from Nain. He claims that this was the first that he had heard that the shroud existed."

Martha paused before sharing more, because she knew that the rest of it would greatly disturb Hadassah.

"He admitted to us," stated Mary in a quiet voice, "that he wants to be buried in the shroud of the Lord so that he will not die again. He shared with us that his experience with dying was not good, although he could not remember much. His memory began more when he awoke in his grave clothes than at any other point of his death."

Hadassah nodded because she had limited memory herself of anything beyond her rebirth.

"That is where you come in," Martha stated, as she startled Hadassah with the choice of words.

"He is hoping that you will agree to make the arrangements once his body is cleansed after death, to ensure that he is buried in the burial shroud of Jesus. He is planning to make a promise to you that he will do the same for you once you die as well," Martha held Hadassah's eyes as she reported it, remembering how shocked she and Mary had been when they first heard it as well.

"My Lord!" gasped Hadassah as she cupped a hand over her mouth.

The plot seemed somehow sacrilegious and she could hardly believe that anyone could even think to conjure up such an awful scheme in an effort to stay alive. She was going to get to the bottom of this, and she believed that the Apostle Peter was the next one she needed to see. She wanted nothing more to do with Josiah, and planned to leave Bethany as soon as she could speak to the Apostle.

All three of the women stood slowly to make their descent back down to the main quarters of the house, and momentarily Hadassah paused to offer her assistance in serving so many guests. Martha considered it for a moment and then declined. Both she and Mary had become completely different women as they matured in years, but one thing had never changed about Mary. She was still no help in the kitchen.

CHAPTER THIRTEEN

Several scribes and Pharisees had just left a meeting with the Apostle Peter, and by the looks on their faces one could see that they left his presence just as disappointed as Josiah. Only theirs was mixed with a good dose of fury.

One turned, just as they exited, to say to Peter, "Old man, we know where you abide here in Bethany, and every time you move those primitive bones of yours to empty your bowels into the stool pot, we know it before you can make it back to your pallet."

Peter was not one who was easily derailed by a barb, and looked back at him not missing a beat to respond, "If my stool pot comes up missing, I will know where to send Eber to retrieve it."

After their hurried and noisy departure, Eber sat quietly watching the Apostle, then dropped his head in his hands in audible exasperation. Though Peter was an old man now, he was just as dangerous to the Pharisees as ever. They were constantly on the move to stay one step ahead of his assassins, but Peter never made it easy for him.

"Father," Eber started, "I wish you would please find a way to be yourself milder."

Peter threw back his head and enjoyed a good belly laugh at that one.

"I am too old to change, my Eber, and they should all know by now that to threaten an old man is futile. Every day that I wake up and I can still take a breath, is as much a surprise to me as anyone!" Peter said it with mischief, but Eber could not smile with him.

Though Peter seldom suffered sickness in his body, Eber worried that day by day he seemed more frail and fragile. He tended to worry more when they had to take to the cobbled roads for a trip, because the end of the journey always meant that the Apostle would need a day or two to recover just from the ride. He could not imagine living without this great man of God in his life, and more often than not wondered what he would do without him.

Peter discerned his thoughts, and reached out to clutch the hand of the only real son that he had ever had. The knock on the door startled Eber, but not Peter.

"What could they want now?" asked Eber in a huff.

"No...it is Hadassah," stated Peter, "there is information that I need to give her. It is good that she has come at this very hour."

Eber could only shake his head at Peter. He had long since given up trying to figure out how Peter knew what he knew. Here they were lodging in the home of a complete stranger, but Peter knew where everything was in the house.

"Quickly, Eber, open the door for her," stated Peter, "time is of the essence."

"Hadassah!" Peter reached up to welcome her in.

"Is it well with you, my daughter?" asked Peter in a merry tone.

"It is well, and I pray that it is well with you also, Rabbi," answered Hadassah.

As she sat before Peter, she matched smiles with him, and felt truly honored at his welcome.

"I couldn't help noticing the group of Pharisees by the way. They were their usual self-righteous selves. They even rebuked me for not covering my face. But I have covered my face for a lifetime. The cover about my head should be sufficient to meet all of the rules and laws of the scriptures."

Hadassah stated it with an uncharacteristic flip of her hand. She decided to adopt this mannerism from Sarah because she liked it. Peter leaned back and enjoyed a hearty chuckle at that. She took a few moments to share news of her meeting with Sarah on the road to Mary and Martha's home, and also shared with him how much she'd learned from the story about his walking on the water to combat fear. Peter nodded at this, for the details as Sarah had relayed them were very accurate.

"Sarah committed me to do a work with those who are poor and infirmed. It is a work that I am cut out to do, and I shall do it willingly for the balance of my days in humility," Hadassah said it in a quiet and sincere voice.

"Yes," the Apostle answered, "Yes....you shall indeed. And the treasures that you lay up for yourself in heaven shall be great. The day will come when our Lord shall reward every man according to the deeds he has done in this flesh, my daughter. And if you are faithful over these things that seem dreary, our Lord shall one day make you ruler over the great things. So work that you may obtain from Him!"

Hadassah nodded at the words of the Apostle.

"Rabbi, please give me your blessing, for I have never had the blessing of my father," she pleaded.

"Eber!" called Peter, "Come at once and bring me the vial of anointed oil."

Hadassah could hardly believe her ears and eyes.

Eber came quickly and helped the aged apostle to his feet. Hadassah started to stand with him, but he waved her to remain where she was. When he came around the table to stand over her, he opened the vial and poured a small amount upon her temple so that it dripped down her face. She reached up and cupped her hands under her chin to catch the overflow. Then the Apostle of Jesus, who had first opened the way of salvation to the Gentiles by preaching to Cornelius and his household, laid both of his hands upon the head of Hadassah and blessed her and commissioned her to the ministry of missions. The power that surged through his hands was electric, and Hadassah buckled under it and fell to the floor. She lay there for quite a few moments bathed in a glory that she had never experienced in her life. When she came to herself, every ache and pain in her body was gone. She felt not only lighter, but younger.

On his part, Peter was sitting there watching her with a steady gaze. When she was able to meet his gaze, Eber ran to help steady her, and offered her a goblet of wine.

"You will find, my daughter," stated Peter, "that there is an anointing upon you to heal the sick and deliver those who are bound by unclean spirits. Even as you feed them and speak comfort to the common people, also touch them to heal their wounded bodies and broken spirits. For this cause, you were singled out to be brought back from the dead. And may the power and grace of our Lord Jesus Christ be upon you in great measure, and to work His good will in you and through you for this good work! May the will of the Lord be done in your life!" declared the Apostle.

Hadassah had just managed to clear her head, and now she was reduced to tears at this blessing. She wept for quite some time, and the Apostle did nothing to stop it. He knew that they were not the tears of a woman, but rather the tears of a newly commissioned disciple.

When she was able to regain her composure, she stepped momentarily from the presence of Peter to wash her face. This weekend was her true rebirth, she realized, and not the moment that she had been brought back from the dead.

"The Pharisees were eager to know what I shared with all of you last night at the home of Eleazar," stated Peter to open up the discussion when she returned to the room.

"Of course, they already knew because they had heard it from Josiah, but they wanted to test me to see what I would say. What they lack in astuteness, they make up for in swatting at gnats. They should have known how I would respond to their demand for information, but perhaps they are too interested in stool pots."

Hadassah was confused about the reference to stool pots, but the merriment in his eyes spoke volumes.

"I am just come from the home of Mary and Martha," offered Hadassah.

"Yes, I know. Josiah was here earlier in the day, but he probably beat you to the house of the sisters of Lazarus as well," said Peter.

Hadassah nodded that his assessment was accurate.

"By now, you should know what Josiah is up to as it regards you," Peter stated it as a question and a point of fact.

"I do," stated Hadassah, "but it does not move me either way. I hardly know Josiah, except for the strange coincidence that binds us together."

At this, Peter leaned forward to make sure that she would hear the emphasis he planned to place on his next words.

"The three of you were never bound by anything, my dear. There never was supposed to be a pact among you. Although the three of you were the only ones raised to life by the Savior, the fact is, he delivered many, many people from grave clothes."

Hadassah just sat and stared at him for a moment to let the words of wisdom sink in. She was astonished to realize the truth of what he said.

"Why did I ever feel the need to bind my life to that of Lazarus and Josiah?" she asked out loud, but mainly to herself.

"Grave clothes," Peter spoke it quietly, knowing that Hadassah would understand its meaning right away.

"What drives any of us to do the meaningless things that we do with our lives?" Peter asked as a rhetorical question.

"The Master taught us many things when He allowed us to walk with Him on the earth. One of the things He oft reminded us is that many are called, but only a few are chosen. Did you ever come to the realization that you died too soon when you were a young girl of twelve, Hadassah?" queried Peter.

The question confused Hadassah because her father had always taught her that when it is your time to die, it is your time and nothing can stop it. She had always concluded that it was impossible to die too soon. Discerning her thoughts, Peter addressed the popular saying.

"If that is true, then why did the Master choose to bring you back?" asked Peter.

The entire line of discussion startled Hadassah, for there were times when she spoke out loud and times when she said nothing, but it never appeared to matter to Peter one way or the other. Most people needed to hear things out loud, but Peter had walked so closely with the Lord, that to hear it was only to confirm what he heard in the Holy Spirit. The older he got, the more he depended on the ears of the Holy Spirit. But few people knew it, including Eber.

"Because He was the Son of God, and had the authority and power to change times and seasons – including the restoration of an ended life," replied Hadassah.

"It is a good answer but not complete," replied Peter as he enjoyed studying the belief system of the daughter of Josiah, for it was the rare opportunity he was afforded to instruct people who had pure hearts.

She was about to smile, thinking that she had won the contest, when she suddenly remembered that Peter himself had raised Dorcas from the grave. Peter chuckled as he watched her, for she was a good student.

"Hadassah, do you believe that every life has a purpose that can either be fulfilled or aborted? Do you believe that to not know one's purpose is to abort it?" asked Peter.

Hadassah would not have thought so before this trip to Bethany, but at that moment she could truthfully say that she had become a believer. She now knew how possible it was to live a life without ever knowing one's purpose.

"I believe that we can get side-tracked, distracted, deceived, even misinformed and that these things can lead to a life purpose that is unfulfilled, yes, I believe that – and then, there are also grave clothes…" she answered carefully.

She let the rest of her thought process trail off. Peter took up her line of thinking.

"There is an appointed time to every life, even as there was an appointed time and purpose for the life of our Lord. When He first started His public ministry, I remember that He would tell people to not publicize the miracles that He did, but to simply go to show themselves to the priest so that they could be declared clean. He understood that things can happen before their appointed time, and that this can short-circuit God's will for our lives. Even when they took Him to hang Him on the tree, I remember that He told them that they did not take His life – but that He was giving His life up as a ransom for many. I did not understand it all then, but I have understood it better by and by."

Peter paused in his instruction to allow Hadassah a moment to reflect.

"I once allowed satan to enter my heart when I rebuked our Lord for talking of death and told Him that He would not have to suffer at the hands of the chief priests and elders – that we twelve would never allow Him to be taken and killed. The Master turned and rebuked the spirit from which I spoke, for He knew what His purpose was for coming in a body of flesh. He could have easily aborted His purpose by refusing to die the death of a criminal on a tree. He had a choice, Hadassah. Although it was appointed unto Him to die so as to save many, He still had a choice. He could have said no. Had He said 'No,' He could have remained on the earth longer and did many great works. But, He would not have fulfilled His purpose – He would have aborted it for another purpose of His own choosing. My dear..."sighed Peter, "one thing I have learned in this sojourn of my life, is that, just because something is good, does not mean that it is God."

Peter stared at her, because this last lesson would be very important for the work that she would go on to do for the Kingdom, and he knew that he would never see her again that side of Heaven.

"Rabbi, you are a wise man," said Hadassah in a quiet voice.

"No, Hadassah. A man has nothing of the Kingdom of God unless it is revealed through the Spirit of God. Of myself, I have nothing…I know nothing. I came into this world with nothing. But I shall leave out of this world with my works following me to the Judgment of the Great Day. I am but a vine, but our God is the husbandman. My purpose is to bear fruit unto righteousness – it is my reasonable service. If, when you look upon me, you cannot tell that I have been with God, then it is possible that I have aborted my purpose."

Peter looked up and beckoned for Eber to bring wine for him and Hadassah.

"When a life comes into contact with the Master, that person must make an immediate decision to leave all in order to follow Him. If that person chooses not to follow, they will be doomed to follow the whims and fancies of a world that is fading away."

"There are some men," continued Peter, "who think that their trade is their purpose. This man that I am describing to you is the man Eleazar. He thinks he was born to peddle fruits and vegetables. And so," sighed Peter, "he tries to be the best peddler of fruits and vegetables that the world has ever seen."

Peter said it with deliberate sarcasm, and Hadassah dropped her eyes momentarily in embarrassment.

"He has never paused to wonder why God would deliver him from the catacombs to peddle trinkets and baubles. Josiah is another such man. Josiah trades in trickery and good fortune. He thinks that he was raised from the dead because Jesus was just passing by, so he has lived his life taking advantage of anybody who can help him get what he wants. Hadassah," the Apostle spoke her name softly, "it must not be so with you."

She nodded when he spoke her name.

"The Apostle Paul once preached a mighty sermon. He said that if Christ was not raised from the dead, then everything that we have believed for and been martyred for is in vain - that we are yet in our sins. He explained that if the only hope we have in Christ is what we have right now, that all of us who are believers are of all men most miserable. What do we yet hope for if He be not risen?" queried Peter.

"If we believe that He rose again and that He committed to us the work for which He became the first fruits, then we must live our lives like we believe that our Lord is expecting an accounting of what He has left in our care! If we live our lives the same as if we never met the Christ, then we live as men who have never allowed the Christ to be risen in us." Peter paused to let his words sink in.

"Rabbi," Hadassah spoke it quietly but reluctantly, for she did not want him to stop.

"Although I am disappointed at the deception of Josiah, perhaps I am the only one who can reach him. If I leave Bethany to avoid him, and allow him to follow the course he has taken, is there someone else who can reach him in time to turn him back to the purpose for which he was brought back from the dead?" pondered Hadassah.

Peter thought on it for a moment before answering.

"Josiah will come around in a few days, Hadassah, but not before he learns a valuable lesson about getting in bed with the devil. Did your father ever tell you the story of Judas? He came out from us, but was never one of us," replied Peter.

Hadassah nodded that she did know of the sad story of Judas.

"Judas thought he was too wise to be taken in by the Pharisees. True, they are not the brightest men, but they are of their father, the devil. Whatever the devil guides them to do, they do, and they believe sincerely that as they use their devices to hinder the onward march of the Church, that they are doing God a favor. Well...Judas agreed to a bargain with the scribes and Pharisees. They paid him thirty pieces of silver to lead them to the Master so that they could take Him by force. Can you believe that Judas betrayed our Lord with a kiss?"

No matter how many times Peter thought on it after all of these years, it could still rankle him in the same way.

"While Judas played them, they played Judas," explained Peter. "We found him days later at the bottom of a ravine, with a broken neck in the noose of a rope, and his internal organs devoured by birds and scavengers."

Calm settled over Hadassah's soul and she quietly released her false sense of obligation to Lazarus and Josiah. She now realized that Josiah had a choice to make, and that the right choice had to come from a pure heart. She was not the one who could get him there, she realized that now. She could only pray that when he got there, as Judas surely did, that it wouldn't be for thirty pieces of the Pharisee's silver and at the bottom of a ravine.

CHAPTER FOURTEEN

The Pharisees thought twice about going into the tomb of Lazarus to examine his grave clothes. It was one thing to break their own laws regarding the dead – although they had done it before and would do it again if necessary – it was an entirely different matter to really not know what they were looking for. There had been so many rumors and stories about Lazarus during his lifetime, that now that he was dead, all of it seemed somehow passé. Still, for the sake of appearances, they wanted it to seem that they had ferreted out any conspiracy that might surround the death.

They were all gathered together at the home of the high priest Elymas when Josiah arrived. Their security detail frisked the old man as if they thought he had a weapon, and then to add further insult to injury, they demanded that he extend his hands to them so that they could be examined. He turned both palms to them first for inspection, and then the backs. They nodded to allow him access to the home of the high priest but not before they shoved him in his side. Josiah was infuriated by the time he was allowed to enter the main courtyard of the house, and had several thoughts of his own about simply leaving. He was met at the door of the house by a servant of Elymas, who then escorted him into a receiving room for guests. About seven of them were gathered there along with an assortment of scribes and elders.

Elymas spoke first, as he could see that Josiah was in a foul mood.

"Is it well with you, Josiah?" he stated in a flat voice.

"I was before I was accosted by your henchmen," answered Josiah.

It was then that Kedar, one of the servants of the high priest, stepped up immediately to threaten Josiah, but then Elymas waved his hand to the sentry to show that he was unmoved.

"We are forced to take precautions that we would normally not have to take. You understand of course," spoke Elymas. Josiah refused to concede and stood glaring at the group which was seated before him. As Josiah looked about the assembly, it seemed evident that they had been there for quite some time.

"Please, Josiah, take a seat," Elymas offered.

"No, I will not be here long, thank you. I have come at your bidding, now tell me what news you desire of me," said Josiah.

"When we spoke earlier in the day, there was information that you withheld from us," replied Elymas, "you told of what the old fisherman Simon Barjona said to the gathering at the home of Eleazar last night, but you failed to mention what you learned from the sisters of Lazarus. We know you held a private meeting with them, because you were observed by several of our compatriots. We would like to know what you gained from them now," the words of the high priest came out sounding like a demand, and momentarily Josiah thought of swearing at him.

If it were not for the fact that he was an old man with brittle bones, Josiah mused to himself, *he would have gladly given them cause to have him beaten.*

"I have learned nothing new that would be of interest to you. I do not believe that Lazarus is buried in the shroud of Jesus at all, and it is clear to me that whatever its whereabouts may be, there is no one still living who has presence of mind to remember where it has been hidden."

Josiah said it in a dry monotone, and the assembled elders could see that he was no longer a willing conspirator.

"It has been all just a bunch of rumors and conjectures," he continued, "Lazarus is dead, he has been buried by his sisters in a burial shroud made specifically for him, and I could find no one who ever recalls hearing him even mention knowing about the burial shroud of Jesus. Even Peter did not name him when he spoke of those who may have handled the shroud," Josiah added.

For a moment, the group before him sat staring at him in silence. They had also reached the same conclusions.

"As for the bones of Jesus," Josiah continued, "that too is no longer a mystery to me. I am a believer. I believe that He rose from the dead as He said, and that He came back in the flesh and was seen of many eyewitnesses. You will not find bones that will prove that He is yet dead, because He rose again with His bones intact."

The game was over as far as Josiah was concerned, and he genuinely did not care what they planned to do to him for his duplicity.

"If you were not an old man, Josiah, and so close to the grave yourself, I would have you beaten for that blasphemy," said Elymas.

"Perhaps in your old age, your common sense has failed you," it was Talmon, one of the elders, who spoke this time.

"Yes...perhaps it has, perhaps it has," Josiah said it in deep reflection.

"Perhaps it is my common sense that I have needed to deal with these many years since I was raised from the dead myself," said Josiah.

For a moment, they all gasped, for in their intrigue, they had forgotten that Josiah himself had been raised from the dead by Jesus of Nazareth. Then too, many of the Pharisees and Sadducees who had been alive at the time of the miracles of Jesus were dead as well. This assembly had of course heard the stories, but had not believed. As Josiah stood before them and gave witness to his resurrection from the dead, they looked upon him with brand new interest.

"Tell me something, Josiah," began Kedar, "what was it like to die?"

He chuckled when he said it to cover his genuine interest, but Josiah was not to be swayed by the ploy.

"Since you laughed when you said it," replied Josiah, "I have no other choice but to suppose that you do not believe that the Savior raised me from the dead."

As he said it, he realized that Peter would have been proud of him for that one.

"You should watch yourself old man," warned Elymas, "for I perceive that there is nothing wrong with your mind or your tongue. If you would stand here in boldness to declare your innocence of any subterfuge, then you should be prepared to give an answer for whatever we desire to hear."

Josiah thought better of saying a cuss word before the high priest.

"Do you believe that I was raised from the dead by Jesus of Nazareth?" asked Josiah. They all stared at him in silence, for to admit their belief was to admit to the supernatural power of Jesus. With their silence, he turned to Kedar. "Since you do not believe that I was raised from the dead, then you will obviously not believe anything I might say about the experience. You want only to mock me. I refuse to answer."

Just as two of the servants of the high priest were about to strike him, Elymas raised his hand again to indicate that they were not to touch Josiah.

"Leave him be," stated the high priest.

"You may leave our presence, Josiah, you have nothing more that we want to hear. Your aid in the matter before us has been useless and has consisted of nothing more than the hearsay and prattle of an old man who should have been hanged a long time ago."

Elymas said it in a flat, emotionless voice referring to Peter, and waved for his sentries to escort Josiah out.

As Josiah made his departure, he wandered for a good time through the streets of Bethany in an aimless manner. He felt that he had completely lost his bearings. His initial plan for joining the burial procession of his brother Lazarus was to bid farewell to the dead. He had never believed the rumor that Lazarus would never die, but had held out some hope that perhaps the rumors about him being buried in the burial shroud of Jesus might be true.

It all seemed pointless now that he had heard from the Apostle who was one of the closest to the Master that the shroud had no healing properties whatever. It was clear as day to him right now, why the shroud had never been brought forward in a public way. It would have been bartered and sold like a magical charm, and the merchandise of it would have contradicted everything the Master stood for. It occurred to him at that moment that perhaps the Master had taken it with Him when He departed for the last time. It just made sense. He would never have wanted His disciples to get off track with things that did not further His cause, and clearly the matter of His burial shroud would have forever been a hindrance.

Josiah felt something begin to break in his spirit. He felt weary from his own subterfuge, and even worse that he had included Hadassah in his schemes. He had found her to be a lovely soul in person, and he now reflected on how vulnerable she seemed. He had lived such a selfish life since his rebirth from the dead, and had not thought much of anything other than how he could make an extra shekel of silver from the re-telling of his much embellished story. As he kept walking aimlessly, he thought of how useless and fruitless his whole life had been. He had not yet come to the point of shame, but he was getting very close.

"Josiah."

He knew the sound of the woman's voice immediately, and turned toward it with a glad heart.

"Hadassah," he replied.

They embraced as old friends would do, and then stood back to smile at each other.

"Where are you headed, Hadassah?" Josiah inquired.

"I am headed to Jerusalem, but thought to lodge the night with friends I have here in Bethany. Will you walk with me for a moment, Josiah?" she asked.

"Of course, my dear, I am in no particular hurry to go anywhere," stated Josiah.

"I know of your scheme," Hadassah said it in a quiet voice and without judgment.

"I am not angry with you, and I am no longer disappointed," she said it as she tried to search his eyes, but he would not meet her gaze.

"Please help me to understand what your intentions were," concluded Hadassah.

Josiah was silent for a long time as they walked, and now he began to experience shame.

He avoided her eyes as he answered her, "I did not have a good experience when I died, Hadassah. I can remember nothing but dark shadows and the terrible odors from my grave clothes when I came back through the chasm. I remember the sounds of the mourners, and the awful squall of my mother, but I do not remember Paradise as being a good place for me. In fact, I do not remember it at all. It was as if I slept through the entire thing," stated Josiah in a sad, plaintive voice.

"Yes, I know," replied Hadassah, and she really did.

"I did not want to die again. How foolish of me. We are all appointed to die, are we not, Hadassah?" asked Josiah.

Hadassah nodded in the affirmative.

"I cheated death once, and thought to cheat it once more. I thought that if I could gain possession of the burial shroud of our Lord that it would have the healing power necessary to raise me from the dead once more. It never occurred to me that it would not make me younger, and that I would still be an old man newly reborn. I would not have stopped the dying process. I would have only succeeded in prolonging it."

Josiah seemed to be talking to himself, so Hadassah listened without commentary.

"When the henchmen of the Pharisees approached me in Nain to gain information for them about the whereabouts of the shroud, I saw no harm in leading them on. I figured that I could produce a shroud and claim that it belonged to the Master and they would believe it. I would then have the real burial shroud unbeknownst to them and in this way my trickery would kill two birds with one stone," explained Josiah.

"What if they had not believed you about the false shroud?" queried Hadassah.

"Would they have cared? Since they do not believe that He was the Messiah, would they have truly cared about the authenticity of the false shroud?"

Josiah couldn't help but reflect upon what a good plot it could have been, but Hadassah was not impressed.

"What finally changed your mind about moving your deception forward?" asked Hadassah.

He sighed heavily to himself, for as he now verbalized the plot to Hadassah, he could see with penitent eyes how imprudent the whole thing had been from the first.

"It was Peter's report that changed my course," began Josiah.

"When the Pharisees approached me about the shroud, no one had thought that there may have been the blood of the Savior still on it. This detail turned my scheme upside down. Surely, Peter would not have lied about this fact. And surely, he would have handled the burial shroud of our Lord as he was one of the first to the tomb. It occurred to me that had Lazarus taken possession of the shroud, or even one of the disciples, the large blood stains on the shroud would have made it a morbid object of revulsion rather than reverence. In the process of time, eventually the shroud would have brought a carnal focus to the brutality of His death, and away from the glorious Advent of His resurrection."

Hadassah looked at Josiah as he said it, and nodded her head vigorously in agreement.

"It was a good thing that He died," offered Hadassah, "but it was better that He rose again with all power and authority!"

They both smiled at this realization.

"It also occurred to me," continued Josiah, "that this is the stuff that myths are born of. I am ashamed to say that I was taken in by one myself," Josiah stated it slowly and carefully, for he was about to reveal the plot that had included Hadassah.

"I thought that it was our Lord's burial shroud that effected the miracle of Jesus' resurrection. I thought the resurrection power was in the cloth. If that was so, I reasoned, then the cloth would be able to raise me from the dead as well. I knew that since the Pharisees were determined to take possession of it, that if it was truly around, they would use every trick in their arsenal to get it. I also believed, as they did, that because of Jesus' love for Mary, Martha and Lazarus, that Lazarus was likely the one who had the shroud."

Josiah paused for a moment, realizing as he now admitted the truth out loud how utterly self serving his plan had been.

"I did not know of your father's connection to Nicodemus until the Pharisees revealed it to me from what they had learned through interrogations. And so, I did not know that Peter was the one that they really suspected of having the shroud, and not Lazarus. It was with that news that it dawned on me that the shroud was only a secondary matter with them. Really what they wanted to do was to revive several rumors about Lazarus as well as the shroud so that they would have legitimate excuse to examine his tomb. They have long since grown tired of the work of the apostles to establish the Church throughout the known world, and have worked unceasingly to stop them from using His Name. They thought to use the bones of Lazarus as a trick to say that they were really the bones of the Master. In this way, they could say that the Master was a normal man like all others, and could not have effected his own miracle."

Hadassah listened to Josiah with great interest, but remained silent so that he could make a full confession.

"I...I...I decided that if I could purchase the shroud from the sisters of Lazarus, that I would then use it to avoid the death experience again. I planned to ask you to bury me in it at the point of my death. I knew that you would understand my fear of dying again, and having gone through it once yourself, that you would not want to die again yourself. I had planned to bury you in it as well, once you succeeded me in death."

Now that Josiah had it all out, it sounded too ridiculous to be genuine. Hadassah looked at him and for a moment said nothing. She realized how hard it must have been to finally own up to his schemes.

"Josiah, I am not afraid to die," she stated.

He stopped in his path and turned to look her in the face alarmed.

"I have never been afraid," she continued, "in fact, I have longed for it since I was brought back from the dead. I am a much changed woman over these past couple of days, and I see things much different now. I no longer see death as an escape from living. I realize now that there is a divine appointment on my life and I do not want to die until I do everything that I have been given a charge to do. Then, I want to die – and not a moment too soon or too late."

Josiah turned once again from Hadassah, and kept walking beside her. Her words were having the desired affect.

"As I shared with you and the others last night, I cannot remember much, but I do not remember bad things about dying," she said.

"Lazarus, like you, however, did not have a good experience. I remember listening to him once when he ministered on one of the hillsides outside of Bethsaida. Someone asked him the insufferable question of what it was like to die," Hadassah made a face as she said it for she knew that Josiah would understand her exasperation at the question which heretofore defined their lives.

"I remember the far-away look that he got in his eyes, as if he were seeing and remembering something that was not very pleasant for him.

All he would say to us that day was that he was glad that he had been given another chance."

Hadassah looked to Josiah to see what his reaction would be for she knew how much he longed to know what Lazarus' experience had been.

"His sisters, Mary and Martha, told me that he shared with them that he did not experience heaven – he experienced the grave, and that it was what he saw in the grave that disturbed him most. They said when they would prod him to share what he saw, he would only say that there was a great gulf fixed between life and death, and that he would never fully be able to express how grateful he was to be given a chance to get things right. He never indicated that he felt pain in the grave, but he did share with them that when you die, your awareness of the living does not end. He said that you could see things, and hear things just as well as you once did when you were alive, but that there were rules and laws that governed the loss of your life and that you couldn't just do what you wanted. He told them that people were very wrong if they thought that death was just nothingness. He explained to us that when you die, a whole new life begins there. He said the most important thing that he remembered about dying was the knowledge of where you would spend eternity, and how it was too late then to do anything about it."

At this Hadassah turned to look at Josiah, for she hoped that her words were getting through.

"He also shared with them," continued Hadassah, "that when he was raised from the dead, he learned from the Master that what he mistook for heaven, was really the grave, and that he hadn't experienced heaven at all."

"Mary once shared with me that this is all he would say, that he flat out refused to discuss what it was like to be called back from the dead. She says he would get a far-away look in his eyes, and that he would only say that when he slid back into his body, that he could only remember the stink of his body mixed with the sweet smell of spices, and that he would never get that mixed odor out of his memory, ever."

Josiah nodded as Hadassah related it, for he knew a lot about that himself.

"Yes," responded Josiah, "I know the scent well."

They now stood in front of the home of one of the close relatives of Jairus, and Hadassah reached out to grab Josiah's hands to bid him farewell. They stood for a long moment saying nothing, for words could never express what this journey into Bethany had meant to them both.

"I never meant to cause you any harm, my dear, I hope that one day you can find it in your heart to forgive an old fool," said Josiah in a quiet voice.

"Please forgive me, Hadassah. I have not made the progress that you have this past couple of days, but still, I am not the same man. I am changed, if only a little," Josiah continued.

Hadassah nodded to him to push back her tears.

"Josiah, my brother, you are forgiven of course. You have done me no harm," replied Hadassah.

"I must find my own way now," said Josiah.

"I envy what you have found for yourself. I only wish that I could have let my own private demons go as quickly as you have. I fear that I am an old man, Hadassah, and that it is too late for me to change," Josiah said it with genuine sadness.

"No, you are wrong," countered Hadassah, "it is never too late to change – not as long as you are alive, Josiah, not as long as you are alive," she said as she squeezed his hands in hers.

"You no longer cover your face," observed Josiah.

"No, I haven't a need anymore. That was my burial shroud, and I am glad to be free of it forever. I refuse to ever cover my face again. If I die before you die, Josiah, please tell those who prepare my body for the burial, not to cover my face. And for heaven's sake, don't let them hire mourners!"

At that, Hadassah turned on her heels and walked the few remaining paces to the home of her family members – alone, but not lonely.

CHAPTER FIFTEEN

Peter was tired but knew that he could not turn in for the night until the last visitor had come and gone. Eber served him supper and they both waited patiently for the knock on the door that finally came at dusk. When it did, Eber looked to the Apostle for a signal to answer, but Peter decided to let the visitor cool his heels for a few moments. As the knock became insistent, Peter lifted his head and nodded to his young servant, indicating his readiness to see the final visitor of the day.

When Josiah stepped into the room where Peter was seated, he felt tired in his soul, and weary in his body. The two looked at each other as if neither looked forward to the exchange but knew nonetheless that it was absolutely necessary.

"You knew that I would return did you not?" Josiah opened the dialog.

Peter nodded that he did.

"I take it that you talked to Hadassah? And that you came clean with your scheme involving her?" queried Peter.

This time Josiah was the one who nodded in the affirmative.

"Good. And she forgave you I am sure," stated Peter in a flat voice.

He decided to see where Josiah would take the dialog next.

"I know that you do not think much of me, Rabbi, but I still don't see that what I planned was so terrible. My experience with death was not a pleasant one, and I did not want to go through it again. I believed with my whole heart that there was healing in the cloth of our Lord's burial," stated Josiah.

"Tell me Josiah," said Peter, "have you discovered the answer to the question that we left off of this morning?"

Josiah paused to remember the question for his memory was not as good these days as it used to be. He nodded as the memory of the question posed to him by Peter came back.

"Yes," he began slowly, "you said to me that once I learned what raised Jesus from the dead, that this would be an important thing for me to know. Is this what you said to me?" asked Josiah.

"It is a fair representation," Peter conceded.

"That is why I have returned to you tonight. I have not found the answer although I have searched and searched for it with all of my heart. If the cloth did not raise Him, then please tell me by what means He raised Himself," stated Josiah in a soft plea.

"He did nothing of Himself. He often told us when He walked with us that He could only do what He saw His Father do. He also told us that unless He went away from us that the Comforter would not come. This Comforter, He explained to us, would teach us all things, Josiah, and guide us into all truth. He would also give us power to heal the sick, raise the dead, and preach this great gospel in every nation of the world," Peter paused to smile as he spoke it, for it had been his life's work.

"It was the Holy Spirit of His Father that got Him out of the grave, and now that same Spirit dwells in us to do the work of the Son and even greater works," replied Peter.

Josiah sat and stared at the old apostle in astonishment.

"I have never heard that there is anyone called the Holy Spirit. Is it therefore a good thing for Him to dwell in me?" queried Josiah.

Peter nodded his head in approval, for Josiah had finally positioned himself to become a disciple.

"You have used many devices, Josiah, to obtain everlasting life. But only one thing is necessary. If you want life that never ends, then what you seek is through the Christ and not His shroud. He is the Resurrection and the Life and He lives and reigns forevermore. If any man be in Him, He shall never taste the pain of the first death. But if any man has not the Son, he shall taste of death twice."

Josiah gave Peter a forlorn look and pronounced, "In my case, thrice."

At that, the two of them leaned back and enjoyed a hearty laugh.

"It is a hard saying, Rabbi, who can receive it?" continued Josiah.

The mood had lightened between them, and he could see that he and the Apostle were no longer sparring with each other. He was tired of himself, and was glad to have the benefit of the Apostle's patience.

"A wise man can," replied Peter.

"Tell me something, Josiah, by what power did our Lord raise you from the dead?" queried Peter.

"By the power given to Him of His Father," stated Josiah in a quiet voice.

"You have said it well," replied Peter.

"Now tell me this," Peter continued, "do you believe that He rose from the dead with all power in His hands, and that He also gave me as well as His other disciples that same power?"

Josiah thought on it for a long moment and could see where the Apostle was leading him.

"Yes, I can see that by being associated with His Movement, I can gain what He was given of His Father," replied Josiah still struggling to grasp certain concepts.

"No, Josiah, you cannot obtain everlasting life by merely associating yourself with what you call His Movement. Judas confused our Lord's purpose with a movement and lost his bishopric as a result," stated Peter.

"There are many movements, are there not?" queried Peter, enjoying the discussion.

Josiah nodded, feeling a bit defensive, and not enjoying it as much as Peter.

"Movements are for combatants and political rivals," Peter continued.

"The Savior taught us that to have eternal life, you must believe that He is the Son of God and that our reasonable service is to disciple others to believe the same. Can you see the difference Josiah?" asked Peter.

"Is it really that simple, Rabbi?" asked Josiah.

"So simple that a fisherman can understand it and believe," said Peter with a twinkle in his eye.

For a long time they simply stared at each other, for Peter could see that Josiah was still trying to weigh one view against another.

"Rabbi," he finally whispered to Peter, "can you tell me what happened to the cloth of our Lord?"

For a long time Peter eyed him, and decided that Josiah was worth the sleep he was losing.

"All of us were in a terrible predicament on the morning that Mary of Magdala came running to us to tell us that His body was missing from the tomb," began Peter.

Josiah sighed gratefully, for this was the story that he had longed to hear.

"All of us, save Lazarus, had forsaken Him in His hour of greatest need. I have long since made peace with my own failures, but for a long time I believed that my denial of Him was worse than what any of the others had done. When she found us that morning after the close of the Sabbath, we were all in mourning together at the home of Lazarus," Peter paused to gather his memory of the events of that day, for he had not spoken of it often.

Peter peered at Josiah wearily as he said the next thing.

"At that time, we too felt that it was but a movement, and that all was lost and our leader dead. We wept and wept until we had no more power to weep, and tortured ourselves with questions about why He had saved others, and could not save Himself. When someone knocked on the door to Lazarus' home, we were frightened beyond words. We thought for sure that someone had gained knowledge of where we were all gathered, and had come to kill us as well."

Eber stuck his head in the door, for he had been listening from the other room, and knew that the retelling would cause Peter a degree of disquiet. Peter looked up and waved quickly to him, indicating that he was unruffled. He continued the story as Josiah leaned in to catch every word.

"The person who knocked at the door of Lazarus pounded and pounded and demanded that we open to her. And when we discovered that it was the voice of a woman, there was one present who stated that he recognized it as the voice of Mary of Magadala. Of course, we opened to her expecting to find her in great anguish, but instead she came rushing in gasping for breath, crying, and trying to tell us some important message all at once. We could take nothing more, and dreaded to hear what this new development might be."

Peter paused again to take a deep breath, for the story was not an easy one to relay even after so many years.

"I was the one who made out what she was saying first. She kept trying to get the words out, 'He is risen, the Lord is risen! He spoke to me and said to me, 'Go tell my disciples that I am alive!' Then she said to us, 'I have seen Him I tell you, I have seen Him in the flesh! He is not dead!' Of course, none of us believed her and we figured that this was nothing but sorrow and grief. She must have dreamed it, we thought, it could not be the truth. And as we doubted, she said it the more, 'He is alive – for I have seen Him – the stone is rolled away from His tomb and I have seen Him for myself!' I tell you of a truth, He told me to come here and to give you the message that He is no longer dead but alive!'"

Peter hesitated for a long moment and Josiah could see that he was caught up in the remembering of it.

"Until the day of her death, we never spoke again of that day…"reflected Peter, "and I am not sure why. Perhaps it was because she never got over the fact that we refused to believe the report of a woman. We had always tolerated the presence of Mary of Magdala in the group of women who followed our Lord. The Master cast seven devils out of this woman, and after her deliverance, she never seemed to be able to fully express her gratitude. When the multitudes would throng our Lord for healing, she as well as the mother of Jesus, and several other women, would help us distribute food, and see to the necessities of those who were too feeble to get close to the Savior to be healed. It was no surprise to me that she was the first one to whom He appeared. After she was set free, she was determined to give her very life for the Master. And that she did – until the day she died!"

Peter took a moment to shake the memory off and was able to pick up the story once again for Josiah.

"Where was I?" queried Peter.

"….you were saying that she told you that she had seen Him and that He was seen of her alive…" offered Josiah.

"Yes, yes I was. I wish I could say that she was able to bring us around in a few moments, but that would be far from the truth. We had just spent the entire Sabbath feeling that His Mission had failed miserably and that we were better off dead for having forsaken Him. We were overcome with unspeakable grief. You cannot understand how much we all loved Him. So when this crazy woman came to the door yelling that she had seen Him alive and that He had spoken words to her to tell us?!!!!"

Peter paused for a moment so that Josiah would get the effect of what he was describing.

"Why it was crazy…how could we believe such a thing? It was impossible – and yet she kept saying it and I could see from her eyes that whatever she had seen and experienced was real!"

Peter said it with another pause for what he was about to share next he knew would answer many questions for Josiah.

"I think both Lazarus and I saw the same thing in her face, but could we dare to believe that such a wondrous thing could be true? All at once, both Lazarus and I took off running to the tomb to see for ourselves, but he outran me and got there first. When he got there, he did not go in, but stood at the door of the tomb staring at something that was within. It frightened me at first until I stooped down to see what he was looking at. That is when I first saw the blood-stained burial shroud of our Lord. While Lazarus stood there looking - I imagine in shock - I ran into the tomb and noticed that the stained burial shroud was in one place and the head napkin had been folded and left in a different place."

"When I handled them, I knew immediately that this was in fact the shroud and head napkin that Joseph of Arimathaea had wrapped the Body of our Lord in. Lazarus recognized it as well for he had been there at the foot of the cross when our Lord gave up the ghost and died. He helped Joseph of Arimathaea take custody of the Body as well as wrap it in that very self-same cloth." Peter paused again as he was coming to the end of the story.

"It is not true that Mary Magdala ever took possession of that shroud, Josiah, for I was the one who took it back with me to show it as proof to the other disciples. As far as I know, she never even had the chance to touch it, for I took possession of it immediately when I ran to the tomb and entered it first before Lazarus. For the record, he never took possession of it either. He later shared with me that at the moment that he saw it He knew that Jesus was the Christ, the very Son of God."

Peter peered at Josiah a long time, waiting for all of the words to sink in.

"Rabbi, I must ask you," stated Josiah, "….what was it that made Lazarus a believer? I believe that the Master was a miracle worker come from God and that no man could have done the works that He did unless that were true. But like Lazarus, though I was touched by Him, and brought back to life by Him, I cannot reconcile my belief that He seemed an ordinary man as I.

What was it that helped Lazarus believe?" asked Josiah in a half-pleading tone.

"He saw the folded, blood-stained grave clothes that our Lord left behind, and remembered the promise of our Lord that after His crucifixion He would rise again on the third day. That day," stated Peter with a knowing smile, "was the third day."

THE END

www.ingramcontent.com/pod-product-compliance
Lightning Source LLC
Chambersburg PA
CBHW032048090426
42744CB00004B/126